ADVANCE P  T0163607

"Mary Kay Stone is the listening ear and counselor that I never knew I needed. Her compassion mixed with God-given wisdom is served up like refreshing water on the days when your heart feels scorched. Without a doubt, her words will lead many closer to the heart of the Shepherd, and to a new season filled with both hope and joy. This is the book that I will give to every person who is facing grief and walking through the valley. If hope feels out of reach, I challenge you to pick up this book and walk alongside Mary Kay, a loving guide who knows the sound of the Shepherd's voice."

—**Paige Allen**, MDiv., Executive Pastor, Pursue Missions

"As a pastor for decades, I longed for a tool to give people in crisis. Mary Kay has written such a book. It is well written. Readable. Most of all, the tips given for 'getting through the valley' are excellent. I highly recommend. A good read for all 'on the journey.'"

—**Dr. Morris Sheats**, MDiv, DMin, President,
Leadership Institute, Inc.

"*Healing Journeys with the Shepherd* carries powerful revelation that could only come from deep places with the Shepherd. This book draws you quickly into His Presence—especially in the rawness of Mary Kay's sharing from her profound pain and loss. As you read, you literally experience his kiss over her life as she shares her journey through the valley. You will forever be impacted by his love and the purposes he has expressed through Mary Kay's life. I find every word pivotal for this hour and where we must go in the healing of our hearts. At our Center, we will be making this practical guide a highly recommended reading for those whose hearts have been shattered by grief."

—**Amy Black**, LPC, Founder and Director,
Gold Monarch Healing Center, Abilene, Texas

"As I read this book of Mary Kay's journeys with Jesus, the good Shepherd speaks hope into the hurting places of my own losses, giving me courage for the future. Are you walking through your own shadowed valley? Read this book. Drink from these wells of wisdom. Invite Mary Kay, who knows the heart of the Shepherd, to join you along your paths to healing."

—**Reverend Dan Boyd**, Fellow Valley-Walker,
United Methodist Pastor for forty years

Healing Journeys with the Shepherd

HEALING JOURNEYS

Shepherd

WITH THE

A Practical Guide
for Grieving Hearts

MARY KAY MCCAULEY STONE

NASHVILLE

NEW YORK • LONDON • MELBOURNE • VANCOUVER

Healing Journeys with the Shepherd

A Practical Guide for Grieving Hearts

Published in New York, New York, by Morgan James Publishing. Morgan James is a trademark of Morgan James, LLC. www.MorganJamesPublishing.com

One section of this book and several journal entries were written by my friend Lynette Watkins, and she graciously gave me permission to share them in this book.

ISBN 9781642797299 paperback
ISBN 9781642797305 eBook
Library of Congress Control Number: 2019946631

Cover Design by:
Megan Dillon
megan@creativeninjadesigns.com

Interior Design by:
Chris Treccani
www.3dogcreative.net

Cover Photo by:
Mark Stambaugh Photography, Alto, NM

Morgan James is a proud partner of Habitat for Humanity Peninsula and Greater Williamsburg. Partners in building since 2006.

Get involved today! Visit
MorganJamesPublishing.com/giving-back

This book is dedicated to my father-in-law,
Bill McCauley, who never locks his door.
His open-hearted love saw us through the tough times
and taught me the meaning of true grace.

TABLE OF CONTENTS

ACKNOWLEDGMENTS

Thank you to all the loving people, who from the beginning of my healing journey until now, made this all possible. I could never list all the names because there are so many. Know that every conversation, every act of love, and every prayer created a life-changing pathway for restoration. Your kindness will be forever woven into the tapestry of my life.

Jesus, my Shepherd: My gratitude begins with him. I spent this book attempting to describe his heart. His goodness is real, and his heart is true. The look of love in his eyes will never leave me.

My precious husband, Doug: You came into my life at the perfect time. Who knew I would find love again sixteen years later? You so courageously honor this part of my story. You never stopped listening, encouraging, and praying me forward. I wouldn't have done this without you.

My dear fellow traveler, Lynette Watkins: You taught me to see the colors of love and the variations of light through shadow. The ability to collaborate with you on this project means the world to me. Thank you for journeying with me in such an honest, strong way. You are my hero.

Charlie and Karin Hamilton: Your faithful friendship and hospitality in the "hippie cabin" made space for the words to actually get from my heart to the page.

Alice Briggs, Nancy LaPoint, and Lisa Thompson: You were my writing coaches! Thank you for patiently teaching this first-time author the writing dance.

Morgan James Publishing: Your entrepreneurial focus was just the right fit for me. Thank you for this amazing opportunity. Thanks, Terry, for encouraging me until I said yes.

Quest Ministries board of directors and prayer team: Thank you for your powerful support in this process. You carried me on the wings of your prayers.

To my sons: Your strong lives and kind hearts remind me of your father. You are more amazing than you know! I am so very proud of the men you have become. My love for you is on every page.

PSALM 23

The Lord is my shepherd;
I shall not want.
He makes me to lie down in green pastures;
He leads me beside the still waters.
He restores my soul;
He leads me in the *paths of righteousness*
For His name's sake.
Yea, though I walk through the *valley of the shadow* of death,
I will fear no evil;
For You are with me;
Your rod and Your staff, they comfort me.
You prepare a table before me in the presence of my enemies;
You anoint my head with oil;
My cup runs over.
Surely goodness and mercy shall follow me
All the days of my life;
And I will dwell in the house of the Lord
Forever (emphasis added).

THE INVITATION

I invite you to come on a journey with me. The Shepherd is here. He is faithful, true, and full of the love you ache for. He knows the way because he has walked this journey himself. While you traverse the hillside down into the valley, his pierced hands are making careful preparations for your arrival. Be assured that he will never drive you through the desert but will lead you with loving-kindness in the perfect timing of heaven.

Come and see. Comfort awaits as you sit by the refreshing stream for hours and listen to the sound of the waters of rest. Raise your head to receive sips of the cool water from his cupped hand. Take long walks through the tender green grass, thinking and listening as your shaking heart begins to calm and open to the Shepherd's touch. Find a pace that works for you, learning simple ways to care for yourself during your trek through the valley. Pour out your pain so that your restoration can begin. Watch the sunrise, letting its warmth soothe your aching soul.

Times of exploration will surprise you. Narrow paths through immense canyon towers will lead you to places you have never dreamed of. And there, hidden in the depths of the crevasse, you will find beautiful gifts to unwrap. Take your seat at the table and taste the goodness of the Lord. He knows how to care for you in the presence of fear and despair. Feel the strength of his hand on yours as you grasp your sword. With the confident instruction of the Shepherd, you will defeat your enemies. Then emerge from the deep valley to joyfully encounter new landscapes full of the beautiful possibilities of restored dreams. Now that you know the heart of the Good Shepherd, learn to tell your story and live in the blessings of your promised land.

This is my story of healing journeys with the Shepherd through the valley of the shadow. It is the testimony of Jesus. Within a span of six years, I walked through the death of my father by illness, my big brother by suicide, and my husband in a camping accident. I never would have chosen to walk through these deep places of pain, but the blessings I gained are priceless. These journeys shook me to the core, but there I found restoring love.

I welcome you if you are on a grief journey yourself, looking for tools to recover from the pain and find life again. Maybe you want to help someone else on their journey through deep loss. I can offer you my own honest story, share some of what I learned, and simply walk with you for a while. This book provides practical life coaching for daily care while exploring the restoration process as described in Psalm twenty-three. I have also included a section of forty daily devotionals drawn from my own journal entries recorded through the valley and beyond. You have permission to read sections as you can in any order. Pick out what you need for the part of the journey you are on. My prayer is that you find comfort, understanding, and strength for your slow, steady steps with the one who loved you first, the one who loves you most— your Shepherd, Jesus.

THE JOURNEY BEGINS

I am sitting here on my back porch on this beautiful day in early summer, wondering how to tell you this story. My experience is so big to me. It is precious and holy and tender in my heart. The birds are chirping, and people are out and about. It is not unlike that life-changing day in early August, oh, so long ago now. It seems like a dream, a different life time, like another world to me. But it was my world and my journey, and it really happened. Everything can change so suddenly in this life. In just a moment, life can take a turn, and your greatest fear is now your reality.

One peaceful Sunday afternoon, my younger son and I were home on a quiet weekend, playing and puttering around the house. My husband and two older sons had gone on a camping trip to the mountains of northern New Mexico with a dear friend. My husband, a great dad, loved spending time outdoors with his boys. We enjoyed camping and hiking, especially in the mountains. Much of my growing-up years was spent in these mountains at my parents' cabin. It was—and still is—my favorite place. So off the guys went to enjoy one last trip before school started. My husband planned to hike with one of the boys while our friend took my other son fishing.

My phone rang, interrupting the relaxing afternoon. When I answered, a man asked, "Hello, is this Mary McCauley?" "Yes,"

I said. He said, "My name is Stephen; I'm an ER doctor in Santa Fe. I am here on the mountain with your sons and husband. There is a storm here, and"—he paused before saying the next words that would change my life forever—"there's been an accident. Your husband was hit by lightning. I am sorry, but he is dead, ma'am."

Shocked, I asked, "What? Is this a joke?"

"No," he said. "I am sorry. But this has really happened. Quite a few people were hiking here on the summit today. I was near your husband and son when lightning hit the mountain. It was a direct hit."

Direct hit ... lightening, mountain ... my mind and heart were reeling! What is happening? Is this real? Where am I? The doctor broke in and pulled me back to the present. "Mary, are you there? The storm is getting worse. I have to get these people off the mountain now. I am taking your son with me to the ranger's station. He is safe with me, but we have to hurry. I will call you back as soon as I can." *Click.* Silence.

I was standing at the kitchen sink, shaking. As I looked up and out the window, I noticed my eight-year-old boy playing happily in the yard. "Oh no," I cried. "Oh no!" *What will he ever do without his father?*

I do not really remember much of the sequences of events after that. Even now, many years later, I am still trying to recover gaps in my memory. I called my mother and my husband's parents. Oddly enough, I do remember that I started cleaning the house. My mother arrived and quietly joined me. We had done this before.

News spread quickly, and people were starting to arrive. We waited together for the doctor from the mountain to call us back and tell us it was all a mistake and that everything was fine. Waiting.

Thankfully, my close friend saw the need to get me to a quiet place. She caught my hand and led me out to the front porch.

As we sat there on the white swing, we were prompted to pray together. In that defining moment, I found myself surrounded by the love of God, which was drawing strength from the well of my spirit, strength I did not know I had. Without thinking about it, I told Jesus how much I loved him and that I would trust him, even now. His response is forever etched in my heart. "I was your first love, and I always will be."

Unexplainable peace blanketed us, peace that would sustain me for all the days to come as I walked with Jesus through the valley of the shadow. We settled into the quiet of the moment with the presence of God suddenly thick and heavy around us. I felt safe.

CHAPTER 1:

My Shepherd

The Lord is my shepherd;
I shall not want (Psalm 23:1).

Permission to Grieve: The Long Goodbye

Why do people say such strange things?

- "I'm so sorry you lost your husband."
- "You'll be fine. Just keep busy."
- "Oh, honey, you'll find someone new."
- "It's been six months; you should be doing better by now."
- And the ever-popular, "You know, God only gives us what we can handle."

The overall message often seems, "If you just keep busy and get on with life, you will find someone new to make you happy." Who knows what will happen to the one you lost? Somehow lost implies that they are hidden somewhere and can be found. And you know what? The truth is, this is *much* more than I can handle! If God is just allowing this to make me strong, it is *way* too much. There has to be more to what has happened than that.

1

Our Western culture has a strange way of dealing with grief or more accurately, of trying to avoid it. Death makes us very uncomfortable because it gives us an opportunity to confront our own mortality, which most of us don't like to think about. It is also understandably very challenging to see people we care about in deep pain. So here we are, suddenly thrown together with friends and family, all of us very uncomfortable with the reason for our connection. When we are uncomfortable, we can say crazy things in an effort to reduce the pain of the moment. Sometimes we run away from the pain as quickly as possible.

I have a friend who was mourning the death of her child. One day, she asked me, "Where have all my friends gone? Everyone seems to be avoiding me. Did I do something wrong?" I explained to her that people generally do whatever they can to avoid pain, even someone else's pain. They do not know what to do for you, so they keep their distance. They excuse this distance by assuming that the grieving person is being cared for by others or that they need their space or privacy. Sometimes those things are true. But if everyone assumes someone else is reaching out, a screaming void of silence can occur where the bereaved is left alone.

The other mistake people make when a friend is grieving is to go to the other extreme and become overly involved in their life. They want to help relieve the suffering of the one they care about and become codependent, trying to protect them and fix their problems. This creates unhealthy relationship dynamics and prevents the grieving person from healing fully and growing strong and confident on their own journey. Boundaries are necessary to keep everyone involved safe and well.

I was very blessed with a handful of friends who watched over me during my valley journey. One in particular was truly on assignment from God during that season. One day, she described to me that she felt as if she were watching me descend farther and farther into the valley. She knew very clearly that she could not go with me. It was my journey with the Shepherd alone. Her job was to watch and pray from the cliff side with great confidence in Jesus's ability to lead me through in his time. I was comforted by that scene that stayed in my mind, knowing that she and others were watching and praying, always available to help when needed but that my journey with the Shepherd was uniquely my own. Thankfully, these friends moved like graceful doves in and out of my days, helping with practical ne\eds, coming by for a hug and a prayer, or sometimes just sitting with me in silence and being present without trying to fix me. I believe that presence is the greatest gift you can give someone in mourning. Never diminish how powerful your presence is in the world—a transforming force of love.

Many often ask, "How long should I grieve?" The answer is simple: as long as you need to. Some cultures have very set mourning periods: three days, forty days, six months, three years. Many cultures allow the bereaved to focus on their loss and do nothing else for that time period. It is as if grieving is the bereaved's main job for a season. I like this idea. The length of grieving time is not a measure of the love a person has for the one who passed away. And while everyone differs in the time they need to truly heal, I think we all need some focused time to do our job of grieving. In cultures with a more stoic approach, a shorter mourning time, and stifled emotional expression, depression and illness commonly result.

I see this often in my counseling office. People push and push, trying to do life in spite of their pain. They often end up reaching out to me for help because everything is falling apart as they suffer from depression, anxiety, chronic fatigue, illness, and other issues.

This tells me that God did not create us to simply ignore our grief. I believe there is always a way to create space for healing. It will mean changing some things—schedules, relationships, jobs, and expectations—to make recovery your top priority. But it is completely worth it. It is the difference between just surviving and really living again.

You are near to the brokenhearted.

Grief is an opportunity for new dreams, deeper love, and the discovery that God is strong enough for both of you. We are, little by little, saying goodbye to a person and a season of life. But more than that, we release our old views of God and our own identity to embrace a new and glorious understanding of greater things.

In the days after my husband's death, many friends called to offer words of comfort. One particular day, I answered the phone and was relieved to hear the voice of my spiritual father, Bob Sewell. He gave me permission to grieve as he assured me of his love for my family and then said something that set the course of my journey. "Mary Kay, the Lord is enough for you on this journey. We are cheering you on. Go! Go all the way through the valley. Give yourself fully to each step. Revel in the sadness, the anger, the acceptance, the letting go, and the realities of new life. Don't miss a thing! The Shepherd is good, and he will lead you well if you let him."

The Shepherd

"The Spirit of the Lord God is upon Me,
Because the Lord has anointed Me
To preach good tidings to the poor;
He has sent Me to heal the brokenhearted,
To proclaim liberty to the captives,
And the opening of the prison to those who are bound;
To proclaim the acceptable year of the Lord,
And the day of vengeance of our God;
To comfort all who mourn,
To console those who mourn in Zion,
To give them beauty for ashes,
The oil of joy for mourning,
The garment of praise for the spirit of heaviness;
That they may be called trees of righteousness,
The planting of the Lord, that He may be glorified"
(Isaiah 61:1–3).

How can I begin to describe to you this beautiful Shepherd who leads us through the valley of the shadow and into new life? John chapter ten gives us wonderful descriptions of the Shepherd, Jesus. In verse eleven, Jesus says, "I am the good shepherd. The good shepherd gives His life for the sheep." The word "good" there is *kalos* in the Greek.[1] It describes that which is noble, wholesome, good, and beautiful. My fellow traveler, I can tell you confidently that this is exactly how I found him to be—completely good!

Early in my journey, I became fascinated with the passage above, Jesus's mission statement that he proclaimed at the start of

---

1   "Lexicon :: Strong's G2570 – kalos," *Blue Letter Bible*, Accessed June 13, 2019, https://www.blueletterbible.org/lang/lexicon/lexicon.cfm?t=kjv&strongs=g2570.

his ministry in Luke four. As I read this passage over for several days, I felt as if he were making a personal promise to me. The promise was this:

"I will bring you good news in the midst of your bad news.

I will heal your broken heart.

I, your Avenger, will set you free from all the enemies that hold you captive.

I will comfort and console you in your mourning.

And I will trade you beauty for your ashes,

I will give you the oil of joy to replace your mourning.

Instead of a spirit of heaviness, I will clothe you in a garment of praise.

I will plant you as a beautiful tree made right again, and I will be glorified."

Today as you read this, Jesus is making the same promise to you. It is who he is. It is what he does. It is his mission in your life, no matter where you are. Our part on this journey is to know that we need him desperately, to humble ourselves and stay close to him, ever positioned to receive his care. Let me rephrase this. The most important thing you can do on the journey through the valley is to position yourself for healing every day. We will explore honest and practical ways to do this throughout the book.

As you begin, take a look at the characteristics of the Good Shepherd on the next page. Keep this list close to remind you of his goodness often. This journey is so precious and powerful, and the Shepherd is better than you have ever dreamed. I want to assure you right now that better days are ahead. It will not always hurt this much. And you have the tender gift of time with the Shepherd to follow your path through the valley in your own way and at your own pace. Sheltered in his strong arms, you just keep living until you come alive again.

Characteristics of the Good Shepherd

1. Loves his sheep and develops a close, intimate relationship with them so that they know his voice and trust him
2. Understands the needs of the sheep better than they do
3. Understands what threatens sheep and what makes them sick
4. Works tirelessly to provide protection and security
5. Leads them to fresh pastures and fresh water
6. Searches out sheep when they stray
7. Defends sheep against all their enemies
8. Provides protection while they sleep
9. Shears them and examines each one for injury or disease
10. Goes ahead of sheep and prepares the path
11. Disciplines and corrects them
12. Comforts sheep when they are hurt or fearful
13. Keeps sheep on the move so that they don't get into a rut
14. Liberally anoints them with oil to prevent disease or to heal an injury
15. Keeps sheep from fighting and hurting each other
16. Cares for, loves, and sacrifices his life for them

You look lovingly at my life.

17. Rejoices in the health, well-being, and prosperity of his flock
18. Will leave the flock to search for lost sheep
19. Experiences great joy in finding lost sheep
20. Carries the lambs close to his heart
21. Gently leads those with young

22. Gets deepest satisfaction from seeing that sheep are contented, well-fed, and safe[2]

---

2   "Characteristics of a Good Shepherd," *dailyliving4jesus*, April 8, 2011, https://dailyliving4jesus.wordpress.com/2011/04/08/characteristics-of-a-good-shepherd/.

My Soul Restored

He makes me to lie down in green pastures;
He leads me beside the still waters.
He restores my soul ... (Psalm 23:2–3).

Care Instructions for Broken Hearts

You will need a few basic tools for your journey with the Shepherd. They will help you with steady, unrushed, long-lasting healing. You can easily forget yourself on this road and stop caring for yourself. Before you know it, you can neglect the simple things that keep you alive and well. A few months after my husband's death, a close friend of mine greeted me warmly one day. She took a loving look at me and remarked, "You've lost weight. Are you eating?"

Am I eating? I thought. I had not thought much about it or thought about my own needs. I was busy trying to make sure my children were fed. In that short exchange, she reminded me of something I had forgotten: I need to eat well! Remember, you are moving toward a goal: to live through this, and one day, honor God, yourself, and your missed loved one by a leading a vibrant life well lived. There are no short cuts, at least none that truly work. Attention to the basics and nurturing yourself will help you grieve well and find your life again.

Think of it this way: if you were recovering after open-heart surgery, you would be sent home with a very specific list of care instructions from your doctor. They might include things like wound care, pain management, diet, sleep and rest, emotional support, and activity and exercise. This care list is very important for the patient and their caregivers to achieve their goal: full recovery.

You bind up every wound.

In a very real way, those experiencing a loss are recovering from heart surgery. Someone very dear is taken away from your heart. Depending on the closeness of the relationship, you can feel a tearing or breaking of the heart, something spiritual, emotional, and physical. If this is you, you are a heart patient. And I want to remind you of the simple things that will help you achieve your goal of full recovery. This journey is so unique to each person, but a few suggestions can help you.

Walk

Take a walk every day if possible. Do what you have energy for, even if it is just to walk down your block and back or take a moment to climb the stairs during your lunch hour. Get outside. Move your body. Stretch out your five senses. As you move, notice everything around you. See the sunlight through the trees. Listen to the birds chirping, dogs barking, children playing. Smell the fresh air and feel the wind on your cheeks. Let your heart stretch a little too. Even a short walk will bring a bit of new energy to your body and soul. You might be able to walk in your neighborhood or at a nearby park. As you gain strength, venture to other places of interest, such as a hiking path or trail in a different part of your area.

Walk alone. Walk with a friend also. A companion can share with you as you walk many days. I had three especially dear ones who would come and walk with me on occasion. They listened to my heart and shared encouragement. Usually, at some point in our walk, we found a quiet place to sit and pray together—priceless! As time went on, other friends knew of my daily walks and sought out time to check on me and hear what God was doing in my life. I appreciated their connection. I also kept close boundaries around myself to protect my progress. Even after a year or two, I had limited physical, emotional, and spiritual energy. I needed to choose well who was allowed into my private world and when. This kept me connected to a few safe and helpful friends. It also protected my alone time, which was a vital part of my healing.

During these daily times alone, I could lean fully into God's comfort and direction. Walking by myself allowed me time to listen to God, to my own heart, and to my body. The movement of my feet carrying me down the pathways helped me to open up and release the physical and emotional stress I was holding. During these times of honest movement, I sometimes gained new insight to a practical challenge or broke through a stuck place of anger or fear. We need time alone to process well and learn to be okay with ourselves.

The year after my husband's passing, I moved our family to a little community just outside the city, a beautiful area with a lake, hills, and a stream. Nature is such an important resource for my mental health. This was a wonderful place to rest and heal. We moved into a small cabin right on the creek. It was perfect. Every day, I walked by the water and hiked near the little chapel that was situated on a quiet hill. It was my peaceful oasis. I watched the wildlife and listened to the sounds of the water flowing over the rocks. I could rest, think, cry, pray. and just breathe.

People on this journey commonly experience God's caring presence as special gifts become symbols of the nearness of Holy Spirit. I had these experiences as well. I had a precious encounter with a dove shortly after my dad passed away. I share more about this later in the book. Whether it's a dove, a rainbow, a fragrance that seemingly appears from nowhere, or other reminder, God has a way of reminding us that he is always near.

At the time I was writing this twenty-five years later, it happened again. And at the very instant I pasted this journal entry into my writing, a beautiful dove landed right in front of me in the grass. Thank you, once again, Father God, for the reminder of your loving presence.

Nurturing Comforts

God created your senses to serve you. They help you reorient so that you know where you are. Nourishing items and activities that feed your senses will bring healthy comforts to your day. Make no mistake, you will seek comfort on painful days. So think about it. Identifying what helps you will keep you from falling into unhealthy habits. Find simple things that comfort you. My friend brought me a vanilla-scented candle. I lit it in the evening to ease me into night time when loneliness was more intense. You might just need to do something to change your energy in the moment. If you have been sitting for a while, get up and move around. If you just experienced a wave of grief because of an exchange with someone who knew your loved one, go home and take a hot shower and put on some music.

If you need some prompts, the following small things can bring relief:

- a warm bath or hot shower
- a favorite coffee or cup of tea
- a fire in the fireplace
- one or several lit candles
- chocolate (my favorite)
- man's best friend (your pet)
- time outdoors
- activity with your hands, e.g., crafts, painting, gardening, etc.
- gym workout
- soothing music (instrumental or worship with messages of love and faith but no sad lyrics)
- essential oils or candles scented with your favorite fragrance and
- time in the sunshine

Every day, I found a sunny spot on my dining room floor. With coffee cup in hand, I closed my eyes and enjoyed the warmth of the sun through the window. My aching body responded in relief as I pressed into the love of God for me. Somehow the sunlight became a tangible expression of the Shepherd's loving presence. I found it became a very essential part of my day.

People often ask what they can do for someone in grief, and it is hard to know what to tell them. Ask close friends for help. Identify small things that you know you used to enjoy and ask a friend for assistance with it.

Sleep

Everyone responds differently when it comes to sleep. Your sleep patterns might change dramatically at certain stages of your grief journey. Remember that you need sleep—and a lot of it—to recover well. Do all you can to allow yourself extra time in your day to rest, even if you do not actually fall asleep.

Teach me to rest.

At times, I slept deeply and did not want to wake up. Other times, I fell asleep for a couple of hours and then was awake. On those nights, I made the decision to lie still and value the rest I was getting, even if I could not sleep. I understand that the night hours can be the most intense and lonely. Remember, God created the night as well as the day. He created it for you to sleep deeply and to dream. I suggest listening to worship music or something calming, such as a fountain or a sound machine. These might help quiet your mind of anxious thoughts while you rest.

While we are discussing sleep, let's talk about dreams for a minute. Depending on what happened in your story, you might dream about your loved one. Most likely, as time goes by, you will dream a comforting dream about them, an encounter of some kind. You might dream that they are near but unreachable somehow. If you experienced trauma, you might have nightmares. You will probably dream about it, so do not be surprised or unduly upset. Your mind and heart are processing all that has happened, and often the only time we are still with our guard let down is when we are sleeping. Before you go to bed, pray and commit your night time to the Shepherd. Declare that Jesus is the Lord over your sleep. Ask him to heal and speak to you as you sleep in his presence. He will. Really!

If you find yourself having upsetting dreams or other ongoing sleep disturbances, address it sooner rather than later. Lack of sleep alone can create all kinds of physical and emotional setbacks and intensify the issues you are already dealing with. Share your experience with a trusted friend and ask for prayer. Speak to your doctor to see what they recommend for you. You might need some medical support for a season. Do not be afraid to admit you need help. It does not make you weak or unspiritual. It just makes you smart!

Breathe

Proper breathing is another helpful tool. When we are stressed, we tend to take shallow breaths. Your body needs the oxygen from full deep breaths. Become aware of your breathing.

Here are three easy suggestions:

1. Just breathe: Sit quietly and close your eyes. Begin to take in slow breaths through your nose and release them through your mouth. That is all you have to do. Do not try to breathe quickly or take extra deep breaths here. Just become aware that you are breathing normally. Notice the sound, the movement, of your chest, how your body feels. Do this for several minutes.

2. Deep breathing: Take in a deep breath, breathing as deeply as you can. When you think your lungs are full, take in just a little more air. Focus on the rising of your chest and the expansion of your diaphragm. Exhale. Relax and breathe normally. Repeat three to six times. This exercise will increase your lung capacity and usually helps me fall

asleep if I am stressed. If you become light-headed, stop and breathe normally. It will become easier as you practice.

3. Box breathing: Imagine you are drawing a box in front of you with your breath. Using a count of three to begin, breathe in 1-2-3 as you picture drawing a line from your bottom left straight up. Hold that breath for 1-2-3 as you picture drawing the line across to your top right. Exhale 1-2-3 as you imagine drawing the line down to the bottom right corner. And rest 1-2-3 as you picture completing the box by drawing the line across the bottom from right to left. Repeat. Breathe, up. Hold, across. Exhale, down. Rest, across.

Many other breathing exercises can be easily found online. Remember to start simply and build slowly. Always check with your health care provider if you have any concerns. I find that breathing helps me to open up my chest a little and choose life in an intentional way. It's small but powerful. Just breathe.

Write

The tool of writing was one of the most valuable activities in my ability to recover and grow in this journey. I wrote as much as I could daily. To be sure, I just did not have the strength some days. But the more I could process through journaling, the better I did. This book was birthed through my crazy daily attempts to make sense of everything I was going through. All the good and bad days were part of this practice. It allowed me to release the pressure valve that, at times, felt so overwhelmingly tight I thought my chest would explode. It gave me an outlet to share my raw feelings and ask the hard questions without worrying about what anybody would think. It gave me a tangible way to dialogue with God about the changing landscapes of my life. And in those words, I heard the sure voice of the Shepherd bringing comfort, understanding, wisdom, and grace. As you can see, I am still writing.

Set aside time in your day to journal. Many of us learned to journal in very spiritual or productive contexts. Put those boxes away for now and just overflow onto the page. Allow all the random thoughts to fill the space. They are already filling all the space inside your head and heart. You might feel some of what I did: a tightness in your chest, brain fog, or repressed emotions—if you let yourself cry, you will never stop. I promise that if you will allow the page to hold some of the weight of your thoughts and feelings, you will eventually find relief, and the tears will slow a bit. If you continue to stifle your emotions and keep everything stuffed inside, your body and soul will pay the price. And I hate to tell you this, but you will leak. All that pressurized grief will find its way out through issues like sickness, poor choices, depression, anxiety, bursts of anger, etc. So go ahead and let it out!

Here are a few tips for your writing time:

- Start with a journal you will actually use, such as a nice journal that was a gift from someone who cared about your journey. You might want to just buy a plain spiral notebook, such as a composition notebook. I like these because they are cheap and easy to carry around. Some people tell me they just do not like handwriting. If that is the case, use your computer for journaling. Writing longhand holds some value, but not if you will not do it. Do what works for you.
- Keep your writing secure. You need to feel safe about what you write so that you can share your thoughts and feelings freely without worrying that someone else will read them. Find a safe place to keep your journal out of reach. If you

are using a computer, make sure it is your own personal computer and password-protect your documents. This is not about keeping secrets. You need freedom to pour out your sadness and even anger without injuring anyone who might read your most intimate thoughts. You need to manage yourself during your recovery. And that is healthy. I find that sharing *aha* moments and insights from my journals with those closest to me can be very valuable but only as I choose and at appropriate times.

- One of my favorite ways of writing is a method I learned from the books of Julia Cameron called "Morning Pages," which is really simple and liberating.[3] "First thing in the morning, settle down in a quiet place and begin writing every thought that comes into your head. These thoughts might be random:
  o "Why did I have that crazy dream?"
  o "What was I supposed to remember for my boss today?"
  o "I need to add eggs to my grocery list"
  o "Why is that fly buzzing in the window?"

Just write it all on the page and keep going, moving your hand back and forth across the page until you have written three pages. Julia calls it "brain drain." It really works! The more you write, the more you release the pressure of all that noisy inner traffic. "Working with the morning pages, we begin to sort through the differences between our real feelings, which are often secret, and our official feelings, those on the record for public display.[4]

---

3   Julia Cameron, *The Artist's Way* (New York: TarcherPerigee, 2016)
4   Ibid.

I find that once I move past the initial distractions, I can write about my life, express my feelings, problem solve, and hear God more clearly. Often my writing will go from random thoughts to questions to sorting emotions and beliefs to prayer. I discover solutions to my problems and gain new perspective. Many days, this little journey ends in worship as I find relief from my struggles and hear the Shepherd speak life to my heart. Oh, it is so worth the thirty minutes or so it takes to carve out a little space for myself.

Resist the urge to go back and read your journal, at least in the beginning. Sure as you do, your inner critic will show up to tell you what you did wrong. Just keep writing day by day. Enjoy the feeling of freedom as your heart room and head room increases. Watch for Jesus everywhere. Writing will make more room for him in your heart.

Did you miss a day? A week? More? Do not beat yourself up. Just carve out your spot and try again today. I could not write for periods of time. I was exhausted, hurting, or just trying to do life. Guilt and shame are not allowed here. Repeat that to yourself: Guilt and shame are *not* allowed here!

In the early days that followed my husband's death, my father-in-law frequently said, "There are no wrong decisions. We will just do the best we can—let grace fill in the gaps—and that is enough." I held tightly to his words, and I will never forget how they freed me. Every new day of this journey, you are allowed to start where you are and do what you can. Grace will fill in the gaps.

I can hear it now. Someone is saying, "I'm too busy for all this. I have to keep life going. I have a family, a job, and many responsibilities. I do not have time to think about myself right now." I hear you. I really do. And here is my response: Pray and ask God to show you what you need each day. He is so great at this, and he knows how to lead you in caring for yourself. Do one good thing for yourself each day.

I had a friend in this predicament. She lost her son in a car accident. Her daughter-in-law was an addict, and my friend had custody of her two young grandchildren. She also worked full-time. She had one time slot in her day when she could be alone: during her lunch hour, which she often worked through. She was worn out: not sleeping, not eating well, and unable to think clearly. I suggested she take her lunch hour and go to a nearby park with a beautiful pond and walking path. "Eat, pray, breathe, and stare at the water," I told her. "Just be at rest for one hour of your day." She did it. She loved it. And it helped her reset and regain some strength. Then she could think more clearly to add other care steps to her routine and better face her many responsibilities.

Sing

I am amazed at the way the Shepherd has taught me to sing during my journey. It is a truly powerful joy that releases praise as an act of my will. Hebrews 13:15 declares, "Therefore by Him let us continually offer the sacrifice of praise to God, that is, the fruit of our lips, giving thanks to His name." I am grateful for the experiences of offering praise to the Lord in all circumstances. But the praise offerings that have come from the depths of my spirit when my heart was in pain are the most precious. These are the times when my praise was a sacrifice. It cost me something to choose to offer it to the Lord when I was hurting, angry, or exhausted. The results are deeply carved rivers of victorious connection with God.

The word *sing* in Scripture has so many different connotations, including to overcome, to cry out, to shout for joy, to rejoice. We sing in celebration, to express sadness, and to declare victory in battle. It can be like the blowing of the shofar; releasing a sound that penetrates darkness, fear, and sorrow; or bringing victory to the deepest places of soul and spirit. Hallelujah!

"Be exalted, O Lord, in Your own strength!
We will sing and praise Your power"
(Psalm 21:13, emphasis added).

Dance

What? Yes, I said dance. You do not have to wait until you feel better because these times of worship can be powerful healing experiences. Let me explain. God worked often through my close friends to prompt me toward new healing steps. One day, I received a card in the mail. I opened it to see one word: *dance.* I thought, *Dance? Are you crazy? That is the last thing I want to do these days.* But something in my spirit said, "Yes, this is exactly what I need."

I was already clinging to my favorite worship music, singing along, sometimes night and day. I liked the slow music but had begun to find some faster songs that gave me energy. I was even discovering some songs that moved me toward warfare prayer for myself and my children. It felt new but powerful and needed. So dancing was the next step. I turned on the music while I was alone in my living room and began to sway to the beat a little. The next time I tried it, I did a little waltz with a scarf in my hands. I was becoming more comfortable and discovering a freeing connection with Jesus in worship.

At other times, I let the strong energy and beat of the music lead me in places of spiritual warfare for myself and my sons. I reached a place where I was considering moving forward in a ministry of my own. As I began to seek the Lord and consider my options, I felt the enemy pushing back in some very real and dramatic ways. Dancing became a way to pray, move, stomp, shout, and overcome those attacks.

One of my favorite memories is dancing with my daddy as a little girl. I stood on top of his feet as he held me safely in his arms and counted the beat of the dance steps in my ear, "One-two-three. One-two-three." And "Back, side, forward, step together." Finding the rhythm of the dance again in my quiet place brought back a feeling of love, safety, and power as I once again found another way to choose life and healing.

Establish Rituals and Routine

Every day can be different on the journey through the valley. It helps to establish a flexible routine. Have a schedule so that you know what to do when you do not know what to do. Meals, rest, quiet time, coffee with a friend, a trip by your favorite drive-through for iced tea, family time, chores, and work outs can give some needed structure to your day and keep you busy. But don't be too busy. Remember, you are a heart patient. Keep it light but somewhat predictable. Then if you have a hard day and need more rest, you can clear the calendar for that day and rest. If you have a job, work with what you have. If your company offers extra days off, take them as needed. Take advantage of any available flexibility. Do not suffer because you are trying to be strong. Steady and purposeful movement through your days will allow more space for those days—I call them lost days—when you just cannot get going.

Looking back on my experiences, I have to be honest and tell you that I had many lost days, maybe even weeks or months, where I was in survival mode. I do not really remember some of those times in any detail. They seem hidden in the shadows of the valley somewhere. I am okay with that. The Shepherd knows where they are and will bring whatever is needed along the way back to my memory. Sometimes I am surprised by a conversation with an old friend or my family when they mention a small forgotten piece of the story. It is usually helpful and triggers my memories in a positive way. I make comments such as the following: "Really?" "That happened?" "We did that?" "God showed up there?" "I had forgotten."

Create Boundaries

I've already touched on boundaries, but I want to further elaborate here. What are boundaries? Boundaries are decisions you make that allow you to respect yourself and honor the resources God has given you. As I said earlier in the chapter, it was my job to guard my heart and energy, choosing carefully who I allowed into my private world and when I did so. Setting healthy boundaries allows you to say yes to what you really want because you boldly say no to what you do not really want or have energy for. It might be hard to make decisions at times. Pray about where you need to set limits in your life with your time, energy, money, relationships, and behavior. Remember, you are not being selfish by saying no to some things for now. You are being smart so that you can heal. In the future, you will be able to do more of what is asked of you if you put yourself first and set some limits now. Most often, we have more choices than we think we do. And people will respect you when you learn to offer them a clear yes or no.

"I have to set limits for my own wellness and even though I may say no to you, it doesn't mean it's even about you. I'm just taking care of myself."[5]

GENTLE CONVERSATIONS

I sit in the green, tender grass beside a mountain stream. I love this place more than any other. The movement of water around the smooth stones creates harmonies in my soul, soothing my frayed emotions and slowing the circles of my mind. I could sit here all day. Sometimes I do. It nourishes my heart and gives me time for gentle conversations with the Shepherd. I know I can talk to him anywhere, and I do. But a few special places have become "our place." Other such places include a sunny window, a porch swing, my cozy bed, the fireside, and sitting beside a friend, enjoying his nearness together.

I have learned to have real conversations with the Shepherd. Each is a heart exchange, expressing concerns, aches, needs, comforts, hopes, and dreams for the future. Can you imagine how gracious our Savior is that he would be so available to us? He loves to talk to us. One of the things that can happen in the valley is that we move from one-sided prayer lists to the give and take of thoughts and ideas, the heart-to-heart sharing of precious secrets. This dialogue is most powerful because talking with Jesus changes your life every time. It is one thing for me to tell him that my heart aches so much, I do not know if I can make it through the next hour, then just dust myself off, dry my eyes, and white-knuckle it

---

5   Dr. Brené Brown, "3 Ways To Set Boundaries," *Huff Post*, December 9, 2013, https://www.huffpost.com/entry/how-to-set-boundaries-brene-brown_n_4372968.

through the day. It is another thing for me to share how I am feeling and then hear him talk to me, sharing that he, too, is brokenhearted over my pain, and he wants me to simply rest in his love for an hour. Now I feel not only understood, but I have a healing step presented to me by my Shepherd that will ease me through.

I know your voice, Shepherd of my soul.

We have a wonderful promise in John 10:4 that we can hear and recognize the Shepherd's voice. Jesus explains, "And when he brings out his own sheep, he goes before them; and the sheep follow him, for they know his voice." Take a look at this interesting fact about sheep. "When it becomes necessary to separate several flocks of sheep, one shepherd after another will stand up and call out: 'Tahhoo! Tahhoo!' or a similar call of his own choosing. The sheep lift up their heads, and after a general scramble, begin following, each one his own shepherd. They are thoroughly familiar with their own shepherd's tone of voice. Strangers have often used the same call, but their attempts to get the sheep to follow them always fail. The words of Jesus are indeed true to Eastern shepherd life when he said: 'The sheep follow him, for they know his voice. And a stranger will they not follow, but will flee from him: for they know not the voice of strangers.'"[6]

Think about it; your heart knows the sound of his voice. You have an instinctive ability to know your Creator's call. That makes meaningful conversations with Jesus possible and worth pursuing.

---

6   "Manners and Customs: Shepherds in the Ancient World," *Bible History Online*, accessed June 13, 2019, https://www.bible-history.com/links.php?cat=39&sub=414&cat_name=&subcat_name=Shepherds.

I often write the conversation in my journal as a dialogue: my question, his answer, my feelings, his feelings. These moments can bring deep healing, ease loneliness, uncover understanding, and solve problems. If you write it down, you will have a reminder of what happened to encourage you as you go along. When you are ready, give it a try. The important thing is to spark heart conversations with the Shepherd, which you can explore through journaling as I previously mentioned.

So how do you engage in these gentle conversations? It is really simple.

1. Find a comfortable place where you can take a few uninterrupted minutes. I like to think of it as an appointment to have coffee with my closest friend. Have your Bible and a journal nearby.

2. As you quiet yourself, think of something you want to tell him about. How are you feeling? What are you thinking? Share one thing at a time.

3. Ask him: "Jesus, what do you think? How do you feel?"

4. Listen for his thoughts to come. They might just appear in your mind, and you know they are not yours. You might think of a Scripture or see a picture in your imagination. If it is encouraging and makes you feel loved and hopeful and agrees with the Word, it is probably him. If you are not sure, ask, "Jesus, is that you?" Often you will hear an immediate *yes* in your heart and mind.

5. Now write down what he said to you.

Conversation Starters

Here are a few questions you can use to get started in your talks with the Shepherd:

• Jesus, what do I need today?

- Lord, what do you want to say to me?
- How do you feel about my life?
- Shepherd, what do you see when you look at my heart?
- Do you love me?
- How do you want to comfort me right now?
- Jesus, how do you see my future?

AS BIG AS ALL OUTDOORS

Have you noticed that in this valley, everything can seem magnified? Of course, the pain of loss is so big and focused. Sorrow, anger, regret, loneliness, and questions are incredibly intense at times. But even small simple things can seem larger than normal. It is like reading everything in large print with a magnifying glass. Emotions, needs, ideas, and everything to do with your five senses take on a work of a different dimension. The nearness of Jesus, the movement of Holy Spirit, and the immense love of the Father become more real, more intense than ever before.

Some of my strongest memories from the valley carry that intensity. I remember

- the comforting fragrance of a shower gel my sister-in-law gave me right after my husband's death. Now that scent would normally be pleasant. In those days, I cried a lot in the shower, but I looked forward to the fragrance that permeated the mist as I washed away the day's sorrow.
- a handful of cards and notes that contained a sentence or even one word that became magnified in my heart and mind as I read it. I do not know why that was, but it was.
- every word, note, and harmony of a Hillsong album that became my worship connection for a while.

- the warmth of the sun as I sat with my Bible in my lap, soaking in the comfort. The words on the page sprang to life before my eyes as they moved through my soul, creating the new landscape of my heart.

"I will worship toward Your holy temple,
And praise Your name
For Your lovingkindness and Your truth;
For You have magnified Your word above all Your name" (Psalm 138:2).

One of the definition of magnify is to assign high value to it.[7] It means to enhance, expand, and enlarge something. It means to elevate, glorify, exalt, lift, and promote. This journey of growth is magnified and accelerated. Things seem larger than life. That reality includes both the good and the bad, the difficult and the glorious. One of those glorious magnifications is *you*. No, really! In your weakness and pain, you are becoming more like Christ every moment—more you than you have ever been before, the strongest, most loving, truest version of yourself. The Shepherd is holding a magnifying lens in front of your life because he knows you. He knows what you are made of, and if you will let him, he will magnify your love, your strengths, your gifts, and your faith. Do you see? It is all becoming larger day by day.

Your love is big enough for my journey.

---

7   *Merriam-Webster*, s.v. "magnify, (v.)," accessed June 13, 2019, https://www.merriam-webster.com/thesaurus/magnify.

In Texas, we have a saying for something that is really big: "as big as all outdoors!" We use it to describe someone's generous heart or even their cowboy hat. It means that it expands farther than the eye can see. That is the heart of the Shepherd. It is more expansive than you can imagine, and he is sharing it intimately with you day by day. Be assured that he is lovingly magnifying your potential, and as he does, the pain and giants you might face in the valley are diminishing and fading from view. In the end, his big love wins—every time.

Gratitude

Disappointment emerges from unrealized expectations. Our hearts become wounded. And I believe that pride and rebellion can easily become the guardians of our pain. We lash out in pain with words similar to the following: "Leave me alone! I don't need anyone! I can take care of myself!" What we really mean is: "I am so hurt and disappointed. I'm afraid to trust anyone again." Have you ever felt that way? I sure have. At times, my heart was so tender, I could not bear the thought of anyone coming near my pain. Oh, but Jesus, my gentle Shepherd, knows just how and when to touch our wounded hearts with his soft hand. And if we listen, we will be aware of his loving invitations to healing.

At one point, the shock and numbness of my loss was wearing off, and I was just beginning to feel the reality of the pain. In my quiet time, the Shepherd led me to Joshua 1:9. Moses had just died, and Joshua was being prepared by God to lead the people across the Jordan River into the promised land. God said to Joshua, "Have I not commanded you? Be strong and of good courage; do not be afraid, nor be dismayed, for the Lord your God is with you wherever you go." Joshua was grieving the loss of his spiritual father and confronted with the task of leading the people on a seemingly impossible journey to a new land.

That day, I felt the same way. I felt the loss of my husband and best friend and was preparing to lead my family across a treacherous river into a new land. So I made a decision. Although I felt weak, wounded, and overwhelmed, I turned that verse into a grateful declaration. Lord, I thank you that I am strong! I thank you that I am courageous! I do not have to be afraid! I do *not* have to be afraid! Thank you that you have promised to be with me wherever I go. I am not alone. I will be very strong and courageous!

This was one of the first of many opportunities to say yes to the healing journey with Jesus. And you know what? He never let me down. I can truly say that he has always treated me with a gentle kindness that endeared me to him in ever-deepening circles of love. Today I can tell you that I am grateful for every disappointment, every tear, every heart-wrenching ache, every angry moment, every question.

I'm not talking about just faking it until you make it. Gratitude is something that takes practice, but it pays off quickly. As a matter of fact, the magic cure for discouragement, rebellion, and despair is gratitude. God designed us for something special here. A grateful heart is the gateway to the presence of God. The smallest thankful prayer quickly puts what's inside us in order. You are God, and I am not. Everything I have is because of your loving hand. My life is sustained by your very breath. Even now, in my pain, you are providing for me. I choose to be courageously grateful.

You are worthy of my love.

As I reflect on my long journeys of loss and healing, my heart is full of gratitude for all that God has done for me and my family. In the midst of pain and sadness, I have learned to find strength through the practice of gratitude. It changes everything. My mother was a part of the Great Generation that grew up during World War II. She experienced the hardships of doing without and sending the men in her family off to war. She told me often, "There is always something to be thankful for." I have finally learned that she was right.

Here's how to practically apply this. Determine to make gratitude a daily practice by writing down three to ten things you are thankful for. Sometimes I have to do what David did in Psalm 142:2 and "pour out my complaint before Him [the Lord]" before I can find my thank you. Once I've expressed my honest struggle, I can let go of it a little and think of something I am grateful for: a roof over my head, a warm bed to sleep in, food to eat, faithful friends who love me. Once I start, my heart shifts and peace comes. Give it a try. Maybe like me, you will find that by the end of your journey, you will have a big, fat hallelujah lodged in your heart that nothing can silence.

"When we focus on our gratitude, the tide of disappointment goes out, and the tide of love rushes in."[8]

---

8   Kristin Armstrong, *Mile Markers*: The 26.2 Most Important Reasons Why Women Run (Pennsylvania: Rodale Books, 2011).

Made Right Again

He leads me in paths of righteousness
For His name's sake (Psalm 23:3).

Right Paths

Journal Entry: God, where are you? Who are you? I thought I knew what I believed, but now it seems everything is turned upside down. I don't know anything anymore. I guess I thought that if we loved you and did our best, you would keep us safe so that bad things wouldn't happen to us. I read my Word now and am challenged by it. I can't figure out how some of the promises I have clung to my whole life work in the middle of this tragedy. Where do I go from here? I don't want to be angry and bitter. I've seen the sour faces of people whose stories turned into bitterness, their eyes empty because of the hardness of hope deferred, their joy stolen. They are heartsick and forever misaligned. I don't understand all this. Portions of the foundation of my faith are in ruins. But I refuse to give up. Somehow your love within me causes my heart to press forward, crying out, "This isn't it! There must be more than this!" Shepherd, I will follow you, no matter what. It is the only choice my heart can live with. So here I am again today. Teach me who you really are, not the second-grade Sunday School Jesus but the Jesus who commands the storm in my heart and calls me beyond the tossing waves with a love I can trust. Realign my heart and mind to your truth. I have to know you—really know you!

This section is about making things right again. When our world is turned upside down, we need his rightness. During our walk with the Shepherd in the valley, we need to realign our experience, expectations, thoughts, beliefs, words, emotions, truths, and actions with the Word of God and the very real experiences of his character. Many times, we will have the opportunity to reconsider who God is, who we are, and how this life really works. I can tell you confidently that this is a good and valuable heart work. It is not easy, but it is so worth it. The alternative is to either walk away from the Shepherd with hurt feelings or to live with a kind of limited, shallow faith, walking the walk but never really completely trusting his intentions. These paths are very special, moving you into parts of the valley you never could have imagined or found otherwise. They are often narrow and wind down through openings you can barely squeeze through. They can also be wide and rocky, requiring a great deal of concentration to keep your footing. But with a little obedient trust, they always lead you to the next good thing the Shepherd has for you.

What are paths of righteousness? First, let's consider the paths. Notice that this phrase in Psalm 23:3 uses "paths"—plural, not singular. I love to hike in the mountains. It is absolutely one of my favorite things. I adore hummingbirds and chipmunks. What can I say? I am just a mountain girl through and through. I usually prefer the roads less traveled. I can get lost for hours, exploring new vistas of summits and pines. Well, I'm rarely lost because of the paths. If I pay attention, deer paths through the forest are easy to follow. But sometimes five or six track paths might be near each other in the wilderness, especially in the valley where animals look for a water source. Which one was I following? Am I going down or up? As many times as the paths lead me to an expected destination, they lead me to dead ends, animal beds, and thickets too dense to trudge through. I admit I have gotten lost a time or two, wandering off under the peering gaze of a mountain lion or onto a steep cliff. Finding my way back to safety alone was very unnerving.

I set my heart on a pilgrimage.

In the valley of the shadow, we need the Shepherd's gracious leadership to know which path is the right one to take. Sometimes we hold onto his belt loops and bury our head in his back, blindly following the movement of his steps through dark and narrow places. Other times, we sense his presence a few feet ahead of us on the trail. We cannot see him clearly. But we can see his footprints in the path and follow them.

When I was little, my father taught me to find my way by following his footprints in the snow. I would take the biggest step I could stretch into and put my tiny foot inside his big boot print. If the mountain snow was really deep, I could stand with both feet inside his footprint. As long as I was in his footprint, I knew I was okay. From that place, I often heard his voice ahead of me, "Here I am, babe! Come this way!" I looked up and stretched into the next step, eventually catching up with him and making my way home.

As I explored the definition of righteousness from several sources, I found words like right-mindedness, honor, true, correctness, upright, honesty, goodness, character, virtue, faithfulness, and blameless.[9] These descriptions sound a lot like the earlier ones when we talked about the Good Shepherd. These paths we follow are pathways of his character, his rightness. He is completely good. He cannot be other than he is. And you are not going to change him. He is the same yesterday, today, and forever. He was who he is before your loss. He is who he is today right in the middle of your valley. And he will be who he is in all your tomorrows. Believe me, he is better than you think he is: more kind, more loving, more just, and more powerful. The greatest discoveries in this place you are in will be better than anything you could imagine. So go ahead, ask the hard questions. And one step at a time, bend your will to his loving hand. Surrender your judgements, even of God, and receive new understanding from the Shepherd.

Jesus explained, "I am the Way, I am the Truth, and I am the Life. No one comes next to the Father except through union with me. To know me is to know my Father too. And from now on you will realize that you have seen him and experienced him." Philip spoke up, "Lord, show us the Father, and that will be all that we need!" Jesus replied, "Philip, I've been with you all this time and you still don't know who I am? How could you ask me to show you the Father, for anyone who has looked at me has seen the Father. Don't you believe that the Father is living in me and that I am living in the Father? Even my words are not my own but come from my Father, for he lives in me and performs his miracles of power through me. Believe

9   *Blue Letter Bible,* "Lexicon :: Strong's H2896 – towb," accessed June 13, 2019, https://www.blueletterbible.org/lang/lexicon/lexicon. cfm?Strongs=H2896&t=NKJV.

that I live as one with my Father and that my Father lives as one with me—or at least, believe because of the mighty miracles I have done" (John 14:6–11 TPT).

Now let's talk about the Father for a minute. It is possible that you are okay with Jesus, your Shepherd, but you are not so sure about Father God. After all, you might think that he is the one who allowed all this to happen. Right? Well, making peace with him about those questions is one of the greatest treasures of the process. I believe God is big enough to handle your real questions about your journey and reveal to you what you need to know. He really is. He can handle your pain, your doubt, and even your anger about this. It is my belief that he loves you so much and is fully invested in your journey and the suffering glory you are experiencing here. He is really the only one who can show you his heart and satisfy the questions that stir in the depths of your soul. My desire is to encourage you to keep talking to him.

What is the secret to handling all this? I am going to tell you right now. Keep the communication lines with God open and flowing, no matter what. Honestly, talk to him about everything you are thinking and feeling. Yes, especially the bad stuff: your doubt, your fear, your questions about his character. He will not be offended. He just wants you to stay connected so that he can show you what you need to know to walk with him in holy love now and in the days to come. I know this takes time and might challenge the way your prayer life has worked until now. But I believe it is the key to making it through the valley of the shadow with full, open-hearted, joyful recovery. Jesus wants to show you the Father. This is why he came. Ask him to show you what his Father is like.

The first Christmas, five months after my husband's death, was so painful. For the first time, I felt anger. I so wanted to give the boys a special holiday. But as we sat in the den with the open box of shiny ornaments in front of us, all I could feel was empty and hurt. I could see in their faces that they felt it too. None of us had the energy to continue. So we set the decorations aside and went our separate ways for the evening. It was all so disappointing.

The next morning, I woke up with a knot in my stomach. I could not wait for the boys to leave for school. I wanted to cry. More than that, I wanted to hit something. My go-to emotion is almost never anger, so this was not a familiar feeling to me. But somehow the Shepherd was leading me through my pain. Suddenly, I had an idea. I picked up the box full of shiny Christmas balls and went into the back yard. Thankfully, they were not sentimental ornaments but just those cheap shiny balls you can buy anywhere. I stood in front of my brick fireplace chimney. I threw one against it and watched it shatter. I felt better, so I threw another one, then another, and another. And with each crash, I felt a force of anger I had never known. "Why God? What were you thinking? What are we going to do? How will I raise these boys without their father? We can't even get through Christmas! This is so wrong! It's not fair!"

Every crash brought out more angry words. And then the tears flowed. Then something very special happened. I looked at the empty box. In front of me, the multi-colored kaleidoscope of the broken ornaments glistened in the sun. With hot tears still streaming down my face, I fell to the ground in a heap. I had expressed and released months of pain, and love emerged from the depths of my heart. "I love You, Jesus! I'm so sorry! Please, please come into this place."

Suddenly, I felt peace wrap around me like a warm blanket. God himself, who had been the object of my anger five minutes before, was now my Comforter. His presence soothed my aching soul in a way I will never forget. Not once did I feel condemned or scolded by him. You see, he knew something I did not: that honestly acknowledging my hurt to him would open the door to a wave of his active love that would bring deeper healing to my heart. The result was the powerful discovery of his righteousness. He is right-minded, honorable, true, correct, upright, honest, good, virtuous, faithful, and blameless. And nothing I could say or do would change that.

YOU ARE HIS NAMESAKE

The Shepherd is lovingly leading you on these paths of righteousness for "his name's sake." What does that mean? The Hebrew word for *sake* is *ma-an* and means *intent* or *purpose*. It is also an adverb that means "on account of."[10] On account of what? This meaning is usually connected in Scripture with his mercy, his righteousness, love, salvation, etc., and is an indication or reminder once again of his character. His name is his character, and his character is his name. So for his name's sake, on account of his mercy, his salvation, and his intentions for my life, he leads me on right paths. His focus is showing me his solid essence and forming his great big character in my little bitty heart.

Ultimately, no matter what season of life you are in, this journey is all about a rebirth. It is an opportunity to leave behind old ways and mindsets and be transformed into the image of Christ in a deeper way. It is a quest to find your true identity, try on your new clothes, and get to know who you are in the world from now going forward. Paths of righteousness are safe places where

---

10 *Blue Letter Bible*, "Lexicon :: Strong's H4616 - ma`an," accessed June 13, 2019, https://www.blueletterbible.org/lang/lexicon/lexicon.cfm?t=kjv&strongs=h4616.

powerful exchanges are made. For me, they are places to confront flaws in my foundation, my personal fears, and the lies that I have believed. I can choose to surrender them to the Shepherd in a free exchange of new strength, truth, and love.

"I will greatly rejoice in the Lord, My soul shall be joyful in my God; for He has clothed me with the garments of salvation. He has covered me with the robe of righteousness. As a bridegroom decks himself with ornaments, and as a bride adorns herself with her jewels. For as the earth brings forth its bud, as the garden causes the things that are in it to spring forth, so the Lord God will cause righteousness and praise to spring forth before all the nations" (Isaiah 61:10–11).

God is so kindhearted about this exchange. When I come to him with my struggles, he wraps me up in his great big royal robe of righteousness. He does not shame or expose me when I willingly come to him. He covers me in his own perfect goodness and keeps me safe. Like exchanging dirty, worn-out garments for clean, new ones, he hides me safely in his love while I relinquish old rags that no longer fit. In their place, he provides me with the beautiful garments of salvation. When all is ready, he removes the protective covering, and all heaven applauds my journey.

ETERNAL TIME FRAMES

A very interesting part of comprehending God's right paths is grasping some of his perspective on time. Now I only have a tiny idea of how this works. This subject, however, has been a very revelatory part of my discovery in the valley. Truly, before the death of each of my loved ones, I viewed time in one way. And with each journey through the valley, I found my understanding deepened and my perspective expanded.

First of all, let's talk about our life span. Experiencing the death of someone challenges what we believe about our earthly and our eternal life. My husband died at the young age of forty-one, barely halfway through his life. The sad consensus from many friends and family was that it was very unfair for his life to be cut short in his prime. But was it? If his life was only seen according to the average earthly life span of eighty-five years, and then he just sits on a heavenly cloud all day playing a harp, it seems as if he missed—even wasted—so much. Why would God allow such a thing? I often wrestle with this when I say goodbye to someone after they lose the all-too-frequent battle with cancer. They were too young to die. What about all the time lost?

But what if we look at their life span differently? What if their life span is not just the expected eighty-plus years but an eternal life span with no end? What if it is so much grander than we can perceive now? I believe God's plan for his beloved ones is in the context of this eternal life span. That means that our eighty-plus years on earth are just an inch on a measuring tape that goes to infinity and beyond. This short life has been described as our internship to prepare us for eternity and the life to follow.

Before I had loved ones on the other side, I believed in heaven from a distance. It was nice idea, a beautiful way of thinking. I could make it up as I went, trying to interpret Scripture or at least other people's thoughts about the Bible. I was mostly creating my version of what I thought it might be. But now, heaven is either a reality or it isn't, and that really matters to me. Where are our loved ones? What are they doing? Are they healed, happy, and truly alive? Are they aware of me and my journey without them? Will I really see them again? What do I truly believe?

We must each come to our own conclusions about these matters as part of believing the goodness of God and making our paths right again. I might not agree with the way this life works sometimes. But that does not change the rightness of God or the truth of his Word. Hear the well-lived words of my father-in-law. "Sometimes we just have to let God be right." Oh, beloved, this is all so much greater than we think it is. And the never-ending capacity of love in the Father's heart is on our side. We can let him be right. Making peace with this can lead us into new levels of acceptance, bringing our hearts home again.

"Life on earth is a dot, a brief window of opportunity; life in Heaven (and ultimately on the New Earth) is a line going out from that dot for eternity. If we're smart, we'll live not for the dot, but for the line."[11]

THE MOST IMPORTANT THING

My husband Billy was an evangelist at heart if there ever was one. That meant that his foremost passion in life was to see men, women, and children come to know Jesus as their Savior. He had a spontaneous and authentic way of leading others to Christ through creative, loyal friendship. Oh, the stories I could tell you. So many wonderful people were caught in his big-hearted friendship: ranchers, business women, jazz musicians, pastors, gangster youths, and precious Mexican children living in the brokenness of poverty. They all experienced what happened when Billy McCauley became their real-life connector to the love of God.

---

11   Randy Alcorn, Seeing the Unseen: A Daily Dose of Eternal Perspective (Oregon: Eternal Perspective Ministries, 2013).

Jesus, I lean into your goodness.

God wants to heal you from the inside out. The most important part of our lives that needs to be made right in the valley experience is our relationship with Jesus as our friend and Savior. Today I want to invite you to a new relationship with Jesus. At this point in your journey, if you have yet to receive him as your personal Lord and Savior, will you ask him into your heart right now? You might say, "But I am in such a painful transition. I still have so many questions about God." May I suggest that this is a good place to start? Jesus came, died on the cross, and conquered death so that you can be comforted and made right again. No matter where you have come from or what you have done on the way, he loves you with a love better than anything you have ever known. This love is stronger than sin, stronger than sickness, stronger than doubt or fear, and stronger even than death. His love for you is very personal. He knows you. He knows why you are here. He knows every question of your heart. And he loves you right here, right now. He is calling you today. Will you answer? If you are willing, pray this prayer with me:

Jesus, I need you. I am so weary of carrying the heavy pain of this life by myself. I have tried and tried to make it all right in my own way and strength, but it is just too much, especially now. I'm sorry, God. I'm sorry I haven't believed or trusted you. Will you forgive me for all the crazy things I've done while trying to run my own life? I confess that I have sinned and desperately need a Savior. I ask you, Jesus, to come into my heart today and wash away the hurt and the pain. Heal me and free me to live again in your rightness, in your peace. I give you my life today. Take it!

Please be the Lord of my heart. I receive your love. I receive your love. I receive your love, right now. In Jesus's name. Amen.

Good job! You might be reading this and thinking, "*What do I do now?*" Here are a couple of suggestions.

- First, find some people who love Jesus and love people. You might have been away from church for a while or never been there at all. It's okay. Ask God to lead you. You might know a Christian coworker. Share your story with him or her. Tell them you asked Jesus into your life and that you need to connect with other believers.

- Next, get a Bible. It is how you nurture your new born-again spirit. You will see how powerfully the words come alive before your eyes.

- Finally, keep talking to God in real-life ways: no religion, just heart-to-heart exchanges. You might want to go back to the section on "Gentle Conversations" in chapter two and give those ideas a try now. "For God so loved the world that He gave His only begotten Son, that whoever believes in Him should not perish but have everlasting life. For God did not send His Son into the world to condemn the world, but that the world through Him might be saved" (John 3:16–17).

FINDING YOUR SONG AGAIN

It has been over twenty-five years now with multiple grief journeys along the way. It still amazes me that when someone precious is plucked from your midst, you never really get over it. You experience great healing and recovery. But their life is always an echoing harmony, playing faintly in the distance behind your song. And yet the Shepherd hears all the songs of your life and knows how to bring them all into resonance, blending the notes into perfect harmony. He does not exchange one song for another. He combines their richness to create layer upon layer of redemptive depth. It works because he places his perfectly pitched love between each layer, each experience. Our lives are like an ever-increasing symphony with each individual playing their part of the song as a unique instrument. Listen to Ray Hughes's description from the book, *The Physics of Heaven.*

Have you ever thought about why there's such a difference between a guitar and a trumpet? Or how about a trumpet and a cornet? What makes a trumpet sound like a trumpet and a cornet sound like a cornet? It all has to do with the vibrations reflecting off different pieces of matter in the instrument. The vibrations coming out of a trumpet are different from those coming out of a cornet. They have a different rate, frequency, or even length. Therefore, a rounder, softer sound comes out of a trumpet and a higher, more direct sound from a cornet occurs.

The sound produced from an instrument has everything to do with the size and texture of the material of the instrument from which it's reflecting. Every instrument ever made is unique, for it contains its own sound. Sound through God's creation becomes individual and therefore, dependent upon the instrument. With our hope for glory—Christ dwelling in us—we produce a sound that's been in us since the beginning of time. We bring to life the full meaning of Emmanuel—Christ with us, Christ revealed in us. "Then it was revealed in my hearing by the Lord of hosts." Christ will be revealed as we hear His sound and release our individual, God-appointed sound as His unique instruments.[12]

When a family or community experiences a loss, each person's song is trying to find where it fits again as it seeks to blend into harmony with the lost one's song still echoing in the distance. Finding the tuning of the heart is a painful effort that will allow the dissonance to fade and the harmonies to emerge. At times, the discord is all you can hear and feel. It creates an irritating hum on the surface of your heart. Reactions to this irritation take many forms: sadness, anxiety, depression, anger, illness, self-harm, relationship challenges, and more. But the main issue is always the same: How do I find the resonance of my life song again? It is an intense and often unrecognized longing in every fiber of your being that requires a tremendous amount of energy because you are constantly moving the setting of your life as you try to retune.

The good news is that the Shepherd knows your song and retuning is possible. God says,

"I will whistle for them and gather them,

For I will redeem them;

And they shall increase as they once increased" (Zechariah 10:8).

God is talking about the regathering of Israel in this passage. But I love the thought of the Shepherd whistling for me to draw me back to his care when I wonder off in the wilderness somewhere.

I hear the song of my Shepherd. My heart is running toward you.

---

12   Judy Franklin and Ellyn Davis, *The Physics of Heaven* (Pennsylvania: Destiny Image, 2015).

Listen for the song of the Shepherd. There, in the background of your consciousness, he is singing your song. It takes time to hear it. You will have to learn to be still, quiet your own singing thoughts, and listen for the song beyond the song. You will know it when it graces your heart. And it will draw you in if you let it, for it will comfort you like a gentle lullaby. As you listen and focus in on its sounds, new energy will begin to grow in you. You will feel the Shepherd's love increasing in your awareness. The story that follows is from my friend Lynette Watkins, who found her song again after devastating losses.

I stood looking at the empty space in the living room, missing my piano, but immediately dismissing the thought. Rebuilding a home was the last thing I thought I'd be doing in my early retirement years. A forest fire took our home and everything we owned just a few years before. A lifetime of accumulated comforts were gone. The rebuilding process had been exhausting, expensive, and tedious. Honestly, I was out of strength to deal with the decisions and desperately trying to remember to be grateful for all the blessings. It seemed to take a conscious effort because the memories replayed in my head. Grief had taken its toll. Not only had we lost our home, but three years later, we lost our younger son, and three months after that, my mother passed away. My heart was filled with an inexpressible groan. In light of losing the people we love, losing and replacing things certainly seemed more of an inconvenience than anything else.

I participated in the process of rebuilding, but in truth, my heart wasn't in it. I have since realized that hope is one of the unexpected casualties of grief, and I didn't dare allow it for myself. Hope means looking to the future, an impossible prospect when facing the all-engulfing and tangible sadness of our loss. So I looked at the void in the living room, telling God I didn't need to replace the piano, reasoning that it had been too long since I had played. I explained to the great Redeemer God that I didn't even know if or how I could play since I was so emotionally damaged. I explained that it would probably be too painful to even consider playing again. Looking back, I think God must be amused at those kinds of conversations.

That night, I was searching online for used household items, and a previous search in the ads popped up from a year or so before when losing our home was all I was grieving. It was for a piano. And there was the piano of my dreams: affordable, only a short distance away, and right in front of me on the screen. I laughed, thinking of my previous prayer and believed God was answering, but I was still reluctant to hope. On the way to look at the piano, I prayed to the Lord that if truly the piano was for me, I wanted to play differently than I ever had before. I wasn't interested in the same song the same way but desired to play by ear, something I had never really accomplished, and I wanted it to be between God and me, like a prayer language. The desire of my heart and a prayer for some time was to play the sounds of heaven in the depths of worship.

So it seems I had prayed an outrageously wonderful prayer that day. And on my way to buy a piano, I prayed it again. "Lord, I am looking for my song. Will you help me find it? But not the song as I've known it before. I want it to be deep and special." If you hang around Jesus very much, you can expect your life to be filled with extraordinary circumstances. The grief I was experiencing was and is powerful, but God is still God, and he knows the deepest desires of our hearts.

The day the piano arrived, I began to play by ear. All my music books had been burned in the fire, so I really had no choice but to experiment with the idea of what I had prayed. Excited, expectant, reluctant, and even a bit scared at times, I played, allowing the Holy Spirit to teach me. Starting with only an established key so I wouldn't have to concentrate on the technical aspects, I began to play sound combinations I knew were beyond me. The sound was soothing and healing. My husband and I were in awe. There was an elegant simplicity about it, and I began to feel myself transformed. No two times were the same. It did not flow from my mind but from my spirit. I thanked God over and over as I sat and played. I knew he was healing both my husband and me, and I knew I was learning a deep trust and intimacy I had not experienced before. My husband asked me to play every evening. and each time I played, our little dog came over and sat by the piano bench quietly. In fact, I had told the Lord that I would watch her closely, knowing that she would respond through her senses and not try to reason away her response as we humans sometimes do. This encounter became a guiding light for my soul.

To say it was always as automatic and as wonderful as I have described would be wrong. Each time I came to the piano, I brought the demands and the emotions of the day along with me. Many times, I began to play, and the great sadness in my heart would prevent me from continuing.

I was constantly fighting with the sorrowful, traumatic memories.

One day, when I was alone with the Lord, I began to play. Before long, the bad memories interrupted me, but I kept playing, fighting for peace and praying for God to help me to forgive and give me relief. The more I played, the more I prayed, and the images of those memories swept across my mind's eye. I asked for help. I told God, "I lay these sorrowful images before you, and I didn't want to see them again." The music I was playing grew louder and bolder until I was literally pounding on the keys. Louder and louder, bolder and bolder, I was fighting for my peace on the other side of God's redemption. My key changed to a minor tone as I forcefully struck the keyboard with no consciousness of what I was doing, sobbing and wailing so hard that I couldn't see. The pain of remembering, reliving, became so intense I didn't think I could go on, but I knew something was happening beyond my understanding. I begged God to replace the mental pictures with a better truth that I couldn't seem to resurrect. Eventually, I couldn't take any more. The pain of the experience had doubled me over, so I stopped, ran to my bed, and pulled the covers over my head. I sensed a miracle had happened.

The next day, I sat down to play, a little apprehensive about what might happen. But the miracle was real. God had done a great and deep healing in me. The music has flowed in peace and healing since, and none of the horrible memories have returned. They have been redeemed. I can't remember them at all. I still grieve and have great sadness, but I find peace in the process and play music not of my own making.

There is a mystery to the love of God. Most of who he is defies logic and cannot be processed the way that we normally process relationships and information. It is love. It is a light shining in the darkness; it always wins, and it's very, very real. Once you have experienced the love that our Lord has for you, no one can convince you otherwise, and you enter each and every new experience with greater confidence and understanding.

There is also a mystery to grief. It, too, cannot be processed the way we normally process information. It overwhelms, obsesses, and always leaves you with a palpable sense of great sadness and even confusion. The memories come and help or haunt but often leave you empty. It is your profound love that has now led to your greatest anguish in the form of grief. Only the Shepherd is equipped to guide you through. For me, he used the piano. He put the desire in my heart years before and then awakened it at the perfect time. He spoke to me in a language that I could understand, and he will do the same for you. The song of the Lord is a personal and reciprocal language. Listen closely, he is singing your song.

LONELINESS

Loneliness. Every person experiences loneliness, sometimes in solitude and sometimes in a crowd. Part of the nature of loneliness is that it brings a feeling of shame. "I feel lonely, so something must be wrong with me. Why am I alone? Am I not fun, cool, or lovable? Doesn't anybody want to be around me?" I want to bring some understanding to this struggle if I can. I first want to share that being alone and feeling lonely are not necessarily the same thing. Have you ever been happy to be alone? Think about the times you enjoy being by yourself.

I am an introvert, so my time alone is very important to me. It is how I recharge the batteries of my soul. I have always enjoyed going for a walk by myself. That way, I can think out loud and talk to myself without anyone questioning my sanity. It is fun for me to shop alone so that I can just meander where I want at my own pace. As a mother with a house full of boys, I loved the odd day that everyone was off to school and work, and I could stay home—*by myself*. Time alone allows us to focus and accomplish tasks without interruption. It also provides space to think, to feel, to sort, and to pray. I believe strongly that it is a vital component to a successful journey through any kind of grief.

Jesus, our Shepherd, will lead us through places of aloneness to help us get in touch with ourselves and to allow our hearts room to feel the aches and questions in our soul. In the midst of his busy ministry on earth, our Lord went away from the crowds to spend time alone and talk to his Father. "And when He had sent the multitudes away, He went up on the mountain by Himself to pray. Now when evening came, He was alone there" (Matthew 14:23). Did you notice that? Jesus was alone, not because no one liked him or wanted to spend time with him. On the contrary, it was because everyone did. And he knew the value of moving into the stillness of aloneness. The stillness of aloneness … doesn't that have a nice ring to it? Sounds like something that could bring relief to a weary soul.

How do we press through our loneliness to reach the contented stillness we need to process and heal?

First, stop cursing the solitude. Our American culture places a very high value on busyness. If we can show that our calendars are full and our phone always signaling, we feel productive, valuable, and wanted. We run constantly, trying to prove our worth. When someone asks, "How are you?" we quickly respond, "I'm just so busy." Beloved, this is wrong in many ways. Our worth is not in keeping every empty spot in our day filled but in allowing the gift of time to teach us that we are deeply loved and valued just because we are. Often we stay busy to avoid feeling pain. "If I just keep moving, I won't have to think," you might subconsciously tell yourself. But the truth is, the pain is there anyway, and you cannot heal what you don't acknowledge. Learning to be still requires that we deal with our loneliness and receive it as a tool that shows us where we need to make peace with ourselves. Missing this work can leave us vulnerable as we search for something or someone to fill the void. My fellow traveler, do not let loneliness drive you. It can be a harsh taskmaster. The enemy of your soul will use it to derail your progress. Fear of being alone is one of the most dangerous challenges in the valley and in life. It can cause you to make horrible relationship decisions. Be aware and smart.

Earlier in the book, I told you about my spiritual father, Bob, who was such an encouragement to me. About a year into my journey, his ministry offered me a retreat in the mountains of Colorado. It sounded wonderful: a whole week alone in my favorite setting. So I happily packed my bag and headed north to find a beautiful cabin well stocked with everything I needed, including a hot tub. I awoke the first day, eager for time to write in my journal, enjoy my Word, and take a little hike in the forest. But as the day passed, I felt a nagging sensation in the pit of my stomach. The next day, it was worse. By the third day in paradise, I could hardly bear it. Loneliness had come to interrupt my plans. It was too quiet, and the nights ticked by in never-ending seconds.

I felt terrible despair. I wanted to pack up and go home. I thought, *This is too hard.*

Then something happened. The Shepherd showed up in my loneliness. His words reached into my heart as he invited me to stay. "This is an opportunity, not for despair but for healing. Come with me into the stillness and learn to know yourself as I know you. I want you to learn to be okay in your own skin. I am offering you a chance to unwrap the gift of deep contentment. If you can summon the courage to press into my invitation now and in the days to come, you will never really be lonely again." I lasted two more days at my little cabin. I felt many emotions and fought battles in my mind. But he was faithful and never let me drown in sorrow or self-loathing.

During that time, he taught me to cultivate the seed of contented love deep on the inside. It has served me so well. I was a widow for sixteen years. Pressing through loneliness into healing has proven to be worth the tearful effort every time. I can truly say that I am okay with myself. I feel loved, valued, content, and connected almost anywhere I find myself. I am not afraid to be alone.

I will keep my heart open.

I encourage you to practice being alone from time to time. Stay home by yourself for an hour or two. Go to a movie or on a walk by yourself. Just press in to a little time alone. As you become adjusted, extend the time. Determine to do your best to connect with the Shepherd, allowing him to lead you on the path. His kindness conquers loneliness. You will find that he really likes you. You will be amazed at what you discover about yourself, and you will like you too.

Oh Lord, who would have ever guessed
that you would store such riches
in a secret place called loneliness?
Who would have guessed that in the soil of loneliness.
you would tuck away
the seeds of contentment?
Help us to see that our loneliness is not a feeling to be cursed,
but a friend to be listened to.
We so fear loneliness that we cram our calendars full of
activities, all designed to assure
that we will not be alone.
And theses distractions become so noisy as they clamor for our
attention that we can't hear you tell us that our loneliness is
where you would like to meet us and remind us
that you love us, and that we are really not alone, and that this
world in not our final home, and that deep inside ourselves is the
cure for our loneliness;
Not out there somewhere.
The cure is inside ourselves because that is where you are.
You would have us look inward and see you at work in our lives
to show us the rainbow through the storm, the light flickering in
the darkness, the smile behind the pain,
the hope inside the grief.
You would open our ears to hear the laughter we thought was
gone, the word of comfort we had turned away, the whisper of
encouragement we desperately need.

You would quicken our hearts to feel the warmth of the sunshine
on our shoulders, the assurance of the hope we have as your
child, the joy of an embrace from a friend.
In our loneliness, Father, you would open our eyes and our ears
and our hearts to the wonders of your grace.
Don't let us miss it.
Amen.[13]

New Creation

Healing from great loss is about the creation and recreation of
the landscapes of your life. Have you considered how will look
like five, ten, or twenty years from now? The process of faith in
your journey requires some adventurous exploration with Holy
Spirit to strengthen your soul. He knows the Shepherd's plan, and
he knows you and how to delight you in a partnership of creativity.

Everything I need I find in you.

The Holy Spirit was hovering or brooding over the new
beginnings of creation. "In the beginning God created the heavens
and the earth. The earth was formless and empty, and darkness
covered the deep waters. And the Spirit of God was hovering over
the surface of the waters" (Genesis 1:1–2 NLT).

Just think about it. You might feel the space left by your loved
one is a formless, empty, dark place full of deep and unknown
waters. But just as he did in the beginning of creation, the Spirit of
God is right now hovering over that space in your life, preparing

---

13   Verdell Davis, *Let Me Grieve But Not Forever* (Dallas: Word Publishing, 1994).

for new life to emerge. We see the same scene in Luke 1:26–35 when the angel Gabriel is announcing the birth of Jesus to Mary. He tells her that she is going to have a baby. Astonished, she asks how this can happen because she is a virgin. Here is his reply:

"The Holy Spirit will come upon you, and the power of the Highest will overshadow you; therefore, also, that Holy One who is to be born will be called the Son of God" (v. 35). The Spirit is taking the same action that he did in creation—hovering, brooding, overshadowing the empty womb of a young woman chosen by God to birth the reality of his redemptive plan into the earth. My friend, the creative work of the Holy Spirit in your life is just as powerful. He is creating new life in you to fulfill the dreams the Father has carried in his heart for you since the beginning. Mary's heart cry to this powerful process was, "I am the Lord's servant. May everything you have said about me come true."

Take a few minutes to imagine the Spirit of God hovering over you now. What does it feel like? Can you feel the love of the Father stirring on your behalf? Can you hear the voice of your Shepherd calling you into new beginnings? Sit quietly in the presence of God and allow your faith to stir your imagination. Feel his goodness at work. " … then God said, "Let there be light," and there was light" (Genesis 1:3).

CHAPTER 4:

The Valley of the Shadow

Yea, though I walk through the valley of the shadow of death,
I will fear no evil;
For You are with me;
Your rod and Your staff, they comfort me.
You prepare a table before me in the presence of my enemies;
You anoint my head with oil;
My cup runs over (Psalm 23:4–5).

Come to the Table

We have rested by the stream and gained strength from quiet moments. We have traveled through the narrow places in the valley, feeling the Shepherd's nearness as we navigated strange pathways down into the lower regions. Now lift your head and look around. You have arrived in another part of the valley, large and spacious. What a relief to be free from the confinement of the small walkways coming down the cliff side.

But as you look around the clearing, you sense danger hiding in the shadows. Suddenly, you feel vulnerable, knowing that your wounds are still tender, and your heart is not yet completely reoriented to the Shepherd's goodness. Your weariness overwhelms you, and once again, you just want it to all be over. "Where are we now, Jesus? Is it safe here? What is required of me in this place?" Your heart beats fast as you notice movement in the shadows. Once again, you hear your enemies' threats whispered in the darkness. "Can you *really* trust the Shepherd? Why weren't your prayers answered? What if you never leave this place? Why is he making you go through this?" Despair, self-pity, and doubt swirl in the battlefield of your mind as you strain to see what is emerging in the distance. "What is that?" you mutter.

Offering you his scarred hand, the Shepherd once again interrupts your thoughts. "Come, I have prepared a table for you."

Every time you see his hands, you are compelled to trust him, so you take hold and walk forward. "A table? Here?" you whisper. "But what about my enemies? Don't you see them moving in the periphery of our steps?"

"Yes, I know." Suddenly, you know that the Shepherd is not only aware of your enemies, but he is personally acquainted with every dark force. You realize the partnership of his suffering once more, and you relax a little.

There is a table before you. Right here in the midst of your enemies, there it is—your table. It is not what you expected at all—as if you knew what to expect on this journey. It is the most beautiful banquet table you have ever seen, spread with all your favorite foods, most admired flowers, and candles. You look down and see that you are wearing fine wedding clothes. You feel anointed and strong, adorned with luminescent jewels that represent the character of the Shepherd. He pulls out your chair, inviting you to sit down. Enthralled with the scene before you, you almost forget the danger of your enemies lurking in the distance. But all you can think about is the generosity of Jesus in this place.

"Are we expecting someone important?" you ask him, doubting this could all be just for you.

With a smile, he says, "No, just you and me."

What a warm and handsome smile he has. You have never noticed it before, so regal, yet familiar, completely engaging. Time seems to stand still as you enjoy your delicious meal. You feel so loved and nourished by all the supply before you. The Shepherd energetically regales you with heroic tales of great battles fought and won. Each moment brings greater strength as his passionate confidence fills your soul. You feel as if you could listen all day, but now you sense something new. In your hand is the cold, smooth grip of your sword. Armor covers your clothes with a shield at your side. The Shepherd's attire has changed as well. Dressed as a king going to war, his eyes blaze with love for you, a fierce power residing in his heart.

Once again, you are aware of the enemies all around. But now it is different. You can see others encircling you. The angels are here: mighty, shining, and ready for battle. "It is time," Jesus says. "Let me teach you the secrets of victory in the valley." He stands up, pulls out your chair, and takes you by the hand. He moves deliberately but unrushed, walking you into the middle of the clearing. Awe fills your heart while you watch the Shepherd move, wielding the most regal sword you have ever seen, made of pure gold with glorious jewels, stunning, sharp but not new. "Watch," he says. "The Word of God is sharp in our hands and in our mouths. It is alive and powerful, piercing even to the division of soul and spirit, joints and marrow. It discerns the movements of the heart. With this weapon in your hand, nothing will be impossible for you. Your strength is increasing, and you will learn to use it well. Now take your sword in your hand, and follow me." (See Hebrews 4:11.)

I hesitate. "Why don't you just get rid of my enemies?" I ask.

"I'm teaching you the art of living in true victory. The art of true victory is learning to battle well and gain authority over your enemies. Then you will know that with my help, you are strong, and their demise will be complete." At first, the cold handle felt intimidating. I had been so weak and weary, barely making each trek of the journey into this deeper place. But pulling the sword from the sheath on my side felt so satisfying as the swoosh of the edge cut the air. Something rose up inside me, a strength I had never known that came from a deep place, the same deep place that earlier contained the wailing cries of pain. At last, a sense of powerful, determined confidence filled me. Like a skilled dancer, I followed the Shepherd's every move with my body and sword. All the while, he spoke words that bathed me in light.

I resist fear. I am teachable.

We are going to take a look at the blessings and the enemies in the valley. But first, take some time to meditate on the powerful words of Psalm 18. See the Lord as the fearless warrior riding on the clouds to rescue you.

I will love You, O Lord, my strength.
The Lord is my rock and my fortress and my deliverer;
My God, my strength, in whom I will trust;
My shield and the horn of my salvation, my stronghold.
I will call upon the Lord, who is worthy to be praised;
So shall I be saved from my enemies.
The pangs of death surrounded me,

And the floods of ungodliness made me afraid.
The sorrows of Sheol surrounded me;
The snares of death confronted me.
In my distress I called upon the Lord,
And cried out to my God;
He heard my voice from His temple,
And my cry came before Him, even to His ears.
Then the earth shook and trembled;
The foundations of the hills also quaked and were shaken,
Because He was angry.
Smoke went up from His nostrils,
And devouring fire from His mouth;
Coals were kindled by it.
He bowed the heavens also, and came down
With darkness under His feet.
And He rode upon a cherub, and flew;
He flew upon the wings of the wind.
He made darkness His secret place;
His canopy around Him was dark waters
And thick clouds of the skies.
From the brightness before Him,
His thick clouds passed with hailstones and coals of fire.
The Lord thundered from heaven,
And the Most High uttered His voice,
Hailstones and coals of fire.
He sent out His arrows and scattered [e]the foe,
Lightnings in abundance, and He vanquished them.
Then the channels of the sea were seen,
The foundations of the world were uncovered
At Your rebuke, O Lord,
At the blast of the breath of Your nostrils.

He sent from above, He took me;
He drew me out of many waters.
He delivered me from my strong enemy,
From those who hated me,
For they were too strong for me.
They confronted me in the day of my calamity,
But the Lord was my support.
He also brought me out into a broad place;
He delivered me because He delighted in me.
The Lord rewarded me according to my righteousness;
According to the cleanness of my hands
He has recompensed me.
For I have kept the ways of the Lord,
And have not wickedly departed from my God.
For all His judgments were before me,
And I did not put away His statutes from me.
I was also blameless before Him,
And I kept myself from my iniquity.
Therefore the Lord has recompensed me according to my righteousness,
According to the cleanness of my hands in His sight.
With the merciful You will show Yourself merciful;
With a blameless man You will show Yourself blameless;
With the pure You will show Yourself pure;
And with the devious You will show Yourself shrewd.
For You will save the humble people,
But will bring down haughty looks.
For You will light my lamp;
The Lord my God will enlighten my darkness.
For by You I can run against a troop,
By my God I can leap over a wall.
As for God, His way is perfect;

The word of the Lord is proven;
He is a shield to all who trust in Him.
For who is God, except the Lord?
And who is a rock, except our God?
It is God who arms me with strength,
And makes my way perfect.
He makes my feet like the feet of deer,
And sets me on my high places.
He teaches my hands to make war,
So that my arms can bend a bow of bronze.
You have also given me the shield of Your salvation;
Your right hand has held me up,
Your gentleness has made me great.
You enlarged my path under me,
So my feet did not slip.
I have pursued my enemies and overtaken them;
Neither did I turn back again till they were destroyed.
I have wounded them,
So that they could not rise;
They have fallen under my feet.
For You have armed me with strength for the battle;
You have subdued under me those who rose up against me.
You have also given me the necks of my enemies,
So that I destroyed those who hated me.
They cried out, but there was none to save;
Even to the Lord, but He did not answer them.
Then I beat them as fine as the dust before the wind;
I cast them out like dirt in the streets.
You have delivered me from the strivings of the people;
You have made me the head of the nations;
A people I have not known shall serve me.

As soon as they hear of me they obey me;
The foreigners submit to me.
The foreigners fade away,
And come frightened from their hideouts.
The Lord lives!
Blessed be my Rock!
Let the God of my salvation be exalted.
It is God who avenges me,
And subdues the peoples under me;
He delivers me from my enemies.
You also lift me up above those who rise against me;
You have delivered me from the violent man.
Therefore I will give thanks to You, O Lord, among the Gentiles,
And sing praises to Your name.
Great deliverance He gives to His king,
And shows mercy to His anointed,
To David and his descendants forevermore."

Isn't that passage wonderful? It has given me strength and perspective over and over again. Keep it handy; mark it in your Bible to read the verses the Lord speaks to you in your situation again and again. Make no mistake, life-threatening dangers are in the valley of the shadow. In this vulnerable, disoriented state of your heart, the enemy of your soul would like nothing better than to catch your feet in the mire of grief and steal your future. But God has already promised you, "I know the plans I have for you, says the Lord, to prosper and not to harm, to give you a hope and a future" (Jeremiah 29:11). His promise is true and contains within it all that you need for fulfillment. Please hear these words, my friend. God is for you. All heaven is cheering you on in this fight. You can do this!

THIS IS WAR

The first rule of warfare is to know the enemy. Paul tells us in 2 Corinthians 2:11 that he is choosing to walk in forgiveness in his community so that Satan will not be able to take advantage of them, "for we [they] are not ignorant of his devices." He devises attacks against us because of the very specific blessings God has for us, according to the gifts, call, and destiny of our heavenly designed identity. And here's what's so great: Satan always overplays his hand because he is so arrogant. So within the areas of struggle are divine clues to the treasures of blessing we will carry out of the valley experience and into the new landscape of life ahead.

Keep this thought in mind as we look at the list of dangers that follows. Can you relate to any of these enemies? Where do you see them in your valley? What are the opposite words for each one?

Dangers in the Valley	Blessings in the Valley
Fear	Love
Depression	Joy
Addiction	Freedom
Self-comfort	True comfort
Ancestor worship	Worship of one true God
Obsessing over deceased loved one	Deeper love for loved one with healthy memories
Self-pity	Hope
Anger at God	Release of pent-up emotions
Sickness and disease	Healing and health
Self-preservation	Trust in God's plans
Isolation	Community
Spirit of death	Abundant life

Global cure or looking for a quick fix	Renewed faith in God's timing
Exhaustion	Rest
Insomnia	Sleep
Survivor's guilt	Release
Looking for someone to blame	Acceptance
Stuck	Growth
Loneliness	Contentment
Broken relationships	Strengthened relationships
Trauma (PTSD)	Healthy response to the current reality
Broken trust	Trust restored
Lost creativity	Increased creativity

"For though we walk in the flesh, we do not war according to the flesh. For the weapons of our warfare are not carnal but mighty in God for pulling down strongholds, casting down arguments and every high thing that exalts itself against the knowledge of God, bringing every thought into captivity to the obedience of Christ" (2 Corinthians 10:3–5).

These days will be justified.

Let's take a little time here to consider your arsenal. The concept of spiritual warfare might be new to you, or you might be a seasoned fighter. In any case, this reminder of the basics will ensure that we are using the weapons provided to us by the Shepherd. You will definitely come through this journey with greater skill for victory if you allow the Lord of angel armies to train your hands for battle. So let's go. We'll use our sword, the

Word of God. Read through these verses aloud, and let your spirit rise up in strength. They will be game changers for you when you feel confronted by the valley enemies.

THE NAME OF JESUS

Remember, just say the name, the most powerful name on earth. When I find myself in a battle, the name of Jesus, my Shepherd, stops the advancement of the devil. It is our safe place to run to. In the name of Jesus, you are free, forgiven, healed, victorious, and loved.

"The name of the Lord is a strong tower;
The righteous run to it and are safe" (Proverbs 18:18).

"Therefore God also has highly exalted Him and given Him the name which is above every name, that at the name of Jesus every knee should bow, of those in heaven, and of those on earth, and of those under the earth, and that every tongue should confess that Jesus Christ is Lord, to the glory of God the Father" (Philippians 2:9–11).

THE WHOLE ARMOR OF GOD

My second-grade Sunday School Jesus, the meek and mild Shepherd, and my middle school Bible study on the armor were only an introduction to the kind of warfare I would endure in the places of deep pain and loss in the valley shadows. I needed a kind and gentle Savior for sure. But I also needed the warrior Jesus, the omnipotent king of Revelation one with fire in his eyes. I needed to know this Jesus who would stand watch at my side when

I was too weak to lift my sword. And I needed a master warrior who would put my sword back in my hand and show me how to wield it with sharp accuracy that surprised even me. Fighting by his side, I gained strength, skill, and authority I had never dreamed of—all the while, knowing I was the Father's precious child.

The following passage powerfully describes the armor God gives us as his sons and daughters.

> Finally, my brethren, be strong in the Lord and in the power of His might. Put on the whole armor of God, that you may be able to stand against the wiles of the devil. For we do not wrestle against flesh and blood, but against principalities, against powers, against the rulers of the darkness of this age, against spiritual hosts of wickedness in the heavenly places. Therefore take up the whole armor of God, that you may be able to withstand in the evil day, and having done all, to stand.
>
> Stand therefore, having girded your waist with truth, having put on the breastplate of righteousness, and having shod your feet with the preparation of the gospel of peace; above all, taking the shield of faith with which you will be able to quench all the fiery darts of the wicked one. And take the helmet of salvation, and the sword of the Spirit, which is the word of God; praying always with all prayer and supplication in the Spirit, being watchful to this end with all perseverance and supplication for all the saints (Ephesians 6:10–18).

Dear one, when the pressure is on, take the time to check your armor. Ask the Shepherd to help you. Ask him to show you if you need to cinch up your armor anywhere. Did you leave your shield of faith somewhere on the road? Did you lay down your sword, the Word of God, and quit reading it because you were frustrated and tired? Are you trying to get through this in your own strength instead of relying on the righteousness of Jesus? Check your armor. It is worth the effort, and you will find relief and protection from the attacks you might endure. Then turn and look at the one whose love restores your hope. He is still by your side and will never leave you.

HOPE VS. SELF-PITY

The women in my mother's family had a tradition of owning a hope chest, usually gifted to them when they married. My mother's hope chest was very dear to me. I could rummage through it, reviewing her memories, my baby shoes, pictures of my brother and sister, and blankets crocheted by her mother. When I married, she gave me my own hope chest. Through the years, I've added favorite memories of my children and their father. I love sharing them with my kids on special occasions. When my youngest son got married, I retrieved a rustic carved wooden cross from the depths of its treasures for him, a gift to his father for his service to the community. My son unwrapped it, and with tears in his eyes, said, "Mom! How do you come up with this amazing stuff?"

"My hope chest is always full," I replied.

I have to admit that at times, in the grieving process, I forgot all about my hope chest. But it was always there, tucked away in the corner of my room, waiting to get acquainted with me again when I was ready. Let me encourage you, friend, no matter where you are on your grief journey, a stash of hope is still tucked away somewhere in the corner of your heart. And you can find it and open it up again.

Hope is the confident expectation of something positive. When we hope, we point our expectation toward something or someone to bring about good. The constant and best direction to point our hope to is God. His love is strong enough to overcome all the tough things we endure in life with nurturing strength that produces faith deep within us. Romans 5:5 gives us a wonderful promise. "Now hope does not disappoint, because the love of God has been poured out in our hearts by the Holy Spirit who was given to us." This tells me that when I feel hopeless, I can ask the Holy Spirit to pour more of the love of God into my heart. Faith works by love. So as I invite him to increase my love level, I find that my faith level rises automatically. It resolves the misdirection of my hope and refocuses my heart in the right place.

Lord, you know I'm prone to wander.
But I will not grieve as if I have no hope.

The opposite of hope is self-pity, one of the deadliest enemies in the valley of the shadow. So much so that I want to address it specifically for a moment. When we experience trauma or loss, we can lose sight of our future. In our pain, we can form a mindset of rejection. We might think, *Why me? Why is my life so hard? No one understands what I am going through. Why won't anyone help me?* We can feel passed by, overlooked, or even entitled. *I have been through so much; I deserve sympathy and special treatment.* Yes, you do—for a while, but not forever.

You see, we might be tempted to stay caught in the muck and mire of this place and begin to form our new identity around our loss. It took a conscious effort on my journey not to fall into the pit of widowhood and victimization. What I mean is that I could have easily focused on my loss and pain and played what I call the widow card. *Poor me! I am a widow and a single mom. This is my story. It's who I am. And by the way, God, you made me like this, so now you have to put up with me.* We accuse God because we feel abandoned. These self-focused, disorienting thoughts can come easily in our pain and weariness. We need to recognize them for what they are: self-pity. The truth is, we are not abandoned, and God knows who we are way beyond the temporary identity of our struggle.

My story has a chapter that contains the experience of widowhood and valleys of grief. It is only a part of my story. There is so much more to it. A healthy self-focus will help with your healing. You can honor where you are and extend compassion to yourself in this difficult place. That looks like many of the topics we are considering in this book, such as the self-care ideas in the chapter, "My Soul Restored." Taking time to rest, going for a walk, or even talking to Jesus are all ways of having compassion for yourself, acknowledging your needs, and honoring where you are on your journey. That is very different from the self-centeredness of self-pity that actually invites more weakness, causing you to respond to your pain like a victim. We all go through painful experiences. And we can all choose how we will respond to what has happened.

Be kind to yourself. Ask the Holy Spirit to help you, filling your heart with the love of God. Give yourself some time to heal. You will if you want to. Show compassion by doing one healing thing for yourself each day. Step-by-step, one day at a time, you will complete this chapter of your story and move to the next. So much good is ahead of you. God is good, and he is already preparing the way for you.

My Cup Overflows

You anoint my head with oil,
my cup overflows (Psalm 23:5 ESV).

New Landscapes

Journal Entry: What is this place? I am looking out across a
landscape that is new and strange to me. I was expecting the
scene to be different, more like the old land I came from. I feel a
little disoriented. But I feel something else, a sense of anticipation,
a stir of new energy to go and see. I want to explore this new world
of mine. As I take another look now, I see a beauty that escaped
my attention before. It is as if the Creator is moving his brush
across the landscape, painting it just for me. I cannot see all that is
ahead of me. But I want to go there with the Shepherd. After all,
we have been through so much together. So many twists and turns.
At times, I have felt great apprehension traversing the valley with
him, but now, finally, I feel happy. Will you show me what you are
creating? Let's go see. I am ready to keep going with you, Jesus.

I really thought that when you went through the valley of the
shadow, you finished the journey and then came up on the other side

to landscape that looked like it did when you went down into the valley. But that is not what happened. By the time I made it near the other side, the landscape was so very different. So much had happened. So much had changed. *I* had changed. Now the valley opened up into a vast new landscape, spread out before me like a beautifully painted sunrise full of promise, inviting me to come explore. Gazing at the colors of this new horizon, I noticed that my heart was already there. It was as if I knew this land, and it knew me.

You might feel a strange calm after fighting some of your battles. An unfamiliar quiet resolve is settling into your soul. It is an odd experience after spending so much time and energy denying, fighting, and even bargaining your way through. But something in you is letting go in a new way. Inside you feel a message change in your heart from "No!" to "Okay." It is as if to say, "This is how it is. I know it now. I think I'll be all right."

You can see the reality of life as it is now that your loved one is gone. But you begin to lift your gaze to the new landscape of your own life that is just in the distance ahead. These times of acceptance bring long-awaited conclusions that release you and allow you to move on. They cannot be rushed and seem to have their own time table. But feeling happy again is healthy. It motivates you to let go of survivor's guilt and complete action-oriented goodbyes you could not handle before. You've made peace with God, your loved one, and yourself. These times of readjustment bring fresh hope into full view. Go with it. Remember, you honor your loved one best by a life well lived.

I hear you whistle across this new landscape.

During the many years of learning to walk in my new world, I realized over and over that the new landscape was created by surrender as I partnered with the Shepherd. There are parts of me here. I recognize them as I move through the new spaces. For the most part, they are the best parts of me: my dreams, my gifts, even the very personal aspects of my design, my personality, and preferences. I like myself because I have seen my reflection in the eyes of the Shepherd. It is a true representation of me, untainted by fear and self-doubt. I feel loved, and I love myself. My love for others is changing too. Now I can love more fully than ever, focusing completely on the other person in front of me without self-protection or reservation. I do not have to worry about other people's outcomes because I have gained such great confidence in the Shepherd. Each one of us must take our own journey with him. He can perfectly bring us to where we need to be if we say yes to him.

Back to the view before me, I can see more and more new possibilities. Ahead of me are seasons of partnership with my Creator, watching our dreams come true. I am strong enough now to travel all the varied terrain: high and low, jagged and smooth, resting and warring, in the deep dark or the brilliance of the light. I am glad that the landscape is new and different. You will be also my fellow traveler. Some day.

COMFORT ZONE

During my journey through the valley, I heard people talk about their comfort zone. They said things like, "Changing my schedule really got me out of my comfort zone," or "I don't like public speaking. It really gets me out of my comfort zone." I often expressed myself to my friends in these typical ways. But here, in this strange new land, it was very different. In despair, I often felt around for the familiar borders of my comfort zones. They were nowhere to be found. Everything was so different. I felt as if I were hanging in midair with nothing tangible beside, below, or above me. I often explored my predicament, asking the Shepherd for his help, realizing as time passed that this new place felt familiar. Now, instead of the discomfort of being out of my comfort zone, an assurance of God's presence suspended me in the new places. A sense of freedom began to emerge in the realization that the restrictions of my old ways were gone, and I could move in directions I had never considered before. It was actually a broad place of freedom within the Shepherd's care.

You watch over my heart.

Listen to the experience of Henri Nouwen as he describes life in the new landscape.

You have an idea of what the new country looks like. Still, you are very much at home, although not truly at peace, in the old country. You know the ways of the old country, its joys and pains, its happy and sad moments. You have spent most of your days there. Even though you know that you have not found there what your heart most desires, you remain quite attached to it. It has become part of your very bones.

Now you have come to realize that you must leave it and enter the new country, where your Beloved dwells. You know that what helped and guided you in the old country no longer works, but what else do you have to go by? You are being asked to trust that you will find what you need in the new country. That requires the death of what has become so precious to you: influence, success, yes, even affection and praise.

Trust is so hard since you have nothing to fall back on. Still, trust is what is essential. The new country is where you are called to go, and the only way to go there is naked and vulnerable.

It seems that you keep crossing and recrossing the border. For a while. you experience a real joy in the new country. But then you become afraid and start loving all you left behind again. So you go back to the old country. To your dismay, you discover that the old country has lost its charm. Risk a few more steps into the new country, trusting that each time you enter it, you will be more comfortable and be able to stay longer.[14]

By now in your journey, you have gained great trust and dependence in the Shepherd. You have been through so much together, finding great strength in your vulnerability and in his love for you. So go ahead. Move forward into the new land, your new country.

---

14   Henri J. M. Nouwen, *The Inner Voice of Love: A Journey Through Anguish to Freedom* (New York: Random House, 2010).

LIVING WATER TEARS

"You keep track of all my sorrows.
You have collected all my tears in your bottle.
You have recorded each one in your book" (Psalm 56:8 NLT).

One Sunday, during a much-needed nap, I had a dream—the kind of dream that is so vivid, you are not sure whether it was a dream or reality. I believe it was a God dream because of the life-changing results that filled me with even greater love for the Shepherd than I had ever experienced.

In my dream, I was, at first, observing a scene from a distance. A beautiful green valley was surrounded by mountains that reminded me of the Swiss Alps, the bright warm sun shining. The crisp, clean air rejuvenated me so that with every breath, I experienced a refreshing burst of life. Every fiber of my being felt electric and fully alive. I had the quiet thought: *This is what resurrection power feels like.* Many people were in the valley, and a sense of great joy permeated the atmosphere as their songs and laughter carried through the air. I moved in closer to the scene, standing to the side of the happy commotion. I could see now a gentle river flowing through the midst of the crowd with someone at the center of attention.

Suddenly, something appeared in my left hand: a clear, glass-like bottle with a cork in the top. I gazed at it with a curious feeling of familiar ownership. It felt precious and sweet to me, and I knew it was mine. My focus shifted to the figure in the center, and I started walking eagerly through the grass toward the crowd. My heart was irresistibly drawn toward this one. *Who is he?* I thought. *I know that I know him.* He was sitting on a beautifully carved wooden chair with the headwaters of the river at his feet. One by one, men, women, and children approached him, lovingly talked with him for a moment, and then … wait! What is this I see? Each one held a bottle similar to mine. And they were pouring out their costly liquid into the river so that its flow gently swelled.

You catch every tear.

It was my turn. I stepped without hesitation toward the one at the head of the river. This was a new place, but I felt no fear, for I knew who he was. I felt him before I saw his face. It was Jesus, my Shepherd. "Oh, it's you!" I fell in his arms, and suddenly time stopped. Everyone else faded away. There in his embrace, I felt completely at peace, satisfied, and fully loved. It was the sweetest moment I have ever known, awake or asleep. A knowing look emanated from his eyes. And as I gazed deeply there, I found that he knew intimately the experience of every tear I had ever cried. In that moment, all memories of my life's pain lifted from my heart as the Shepherd's affection for my life opened windows of heaven within my soul.

Now I was aware of the bottle in my hand, and I knew. It was my tears, the tears he had collected in every ounce of sadness and each aching, painful moment of my life. The Son of God had saved each one in love and retuned them to me for a purpose. Standing there in his presence, I opened my bottle and began to pour the tears on his feet. As I did so, everyone there began to cheer and call my name, the sound swelling with an honor I had never heard before. I looked at the Shepherd, who was gazing back at me with tender, loving pride. Joy radiated inside me and then exploded in dance. Jesus stood, and we all began to splash with joy, dancing in the river of living water formed by our tears.

I woke up with a peaceful knowing, a deep experiential assurance of the Shepherd's opinion of my pain. He understands. He not only understands; he cares enough to treasure every single tear and turn them all into a river of living water. What happens to all that water? I believe it flows through us and then out to others through our faith journey. Our words, the telling of our story, help someone else. It might be as simple as a deeply joyful glance or the power of our presence as we weep with a hurting friend. In its time, if you let it, the river will flow, and it will be the most beautiful sight you have ever seen. "He who believes in Me, as the Scripture has said, out of his heart will flow rivers of living water" (John 7:38).

LIVING FROM THE OVERFLOW

New energy for life is emerging in you. You have not felt its flow for a very long time. But now the reservoir of your heart is filling up again. Can you feel it? It is more than just making life work in your own strength or, as we would say in Texas, pulling yourself up by your bootstraps. You have a new connection to someone and something much greater than you: your Shepherd, your strength, and your song. His Spirit within you fills your heart to the brim with resurrection power.

You likely felt the extremes of desolate emptiness as well as expanding fullness on your road to healing. I can tell you I never knew the depths of my own soul until I walked through this journey. And each pathway caused me to explore the vast spaces within: galleries of faith, emotion, belief systems, habits, ways of doing life, the unique rhythms of my heart. Each trek through grief is an opportunity to become better acquainted with your own depths. Of course, it usually begins with the groanings of sorrow—at times, so deep and painful—as we begin to embrace the long goodbye. But now, if you traveled closely with the Shepherd, comfort and new life grows in the caverns of your soul. The discovery of the great capacity within your being, guided by your loving Creator, is one of the most valuable treasures you carry with you from your quest.

Listen to the following description.

And I pray that he would unveil within you the unlimited riches of his glory and favor until supernatural strength floods your innermost being with his divine might and explosive power. Then, by constantly using your faith, the life of Christ will be released deep inside you, and the resting place of his love will become the very source and root of your life. Then you will be empowered to discover what every holy one experiences—the great magnitude of the astonishing love of Christ in all its dimensions. How deeply intimate and far-reaching is his love! How enduring and inclusive it is! Endless love beyond measurement that transcends our understanding—this extravagant love pours into you until you are filled to overflowing with the fullness of God!" (Ephesians 3:16–19 TPT).

The blessing of fullness is overflow. The immense volume of newly recovered compassion, wisdom, understanding, grace, and power-filled faith spills out into the lives of people around us. What a beautiful outcome. New victories are won again and again in the ability to journey with others through tough times, allowing them to laugh, cry, question, stomp, and dance their way into the Shepherd's arms. You will love this part. No pressure—simply do what the Lord leads.

Nothing is impossible.

One day, I was struggling to understand how to work through a tough decision I was trying to make. My friend said to me, "I have complete confidence in you and the Lord and in your ability to do all that he has planned." What encouragement. She offered me supporting assurance that has stayed with me all these years. Now it brings me so much joy to say those powerful words to others. I am confident in your and the Shepherd's ability to walk through this place to accomplish all the great things he has planned. It is part of the overflow of my heart, a free-flowing stream that waters other travelers who cross my path.

TELL YOUR STORY

One day, a few months into my journey, I received a precious phone call from an old high school friend now serving as a missionary in Africa. She shared that the tribes she lived near considered every death a holy event as if God himself had come for a personal visit. She said that if God came to visit, everyone would talk about it, telling the amazing story to everyone they could. And everyone in the community would be eager to hear every detail of the special day. "That is how the people here respond when there is a death in their tribe. They cling together to weep and dance and laugh and share food. But most of all, to tell the story. Over and over again, they tell the story of the visitation and the experience of the one who died. Everywhere you go, everyone you meet, it is the same: 'Please, tell me the story again.'" Her lovely advice that day was to tell the story—over and over again. She said, "Every time you tell it, your healing goes a little deeper."

It has not been easy—telling the story. In the beginning, everyone was talking about it, mostly behind my back. But over time, as I shared bits and pieces, it became a little easier. For months, even years, my family did not talk about the story with each other, trying to ease the pain that was constantly throbbing just under the surface. Even now, as I write this, I feel a little tenuous about telling the story again. But I believe very strongly that we overcome by the word of our testimony (Revelation 12:11) and that my friend was right in her advice. I have experienced healing every time I have shared our story, and I am grateful for the opportunities.

In the valley, you gain the deep knowing that you made it through the heartache and survived well. You become a part of a new community. Willingly or not, you are now among those who know. You now have that look in your eyes and depth in your soul that is recognizable to others who know the valley journey. Whatever event caused your journey, you now share a common bond of facing your greatest fears in the dark night of the soul and finding yourself in the loving reflection of the Shepherd's eyes. As time completes its work in the Creator's hands, a quiet confidence grows strong on the inside, and you *know* that you *know*. And others who know, know that you know. It is a special place of fellowship, the fellowship of suffering in the Shepherd's care. One blessing is that once you know, you can never un-know.

You're the writer of my story.

While it is important to tell your story as you can, treat it and the tender heart that carries it as holy and precious. That means that you have the right and the responsibility to choose well how and when you share and even who you share with. Some people in your world might push you too quickly to use your story to help others. Make no mistake; your story will help others. It is part of the innate kingdom make-up of the experience. But you and the Shepherd get to choose together those times and people. He does not want you uncovered and exposed when your wounds are still raw or when those hearing will not value what you offer. Every time you share, you bring an offering to the Lord, who so graciously carried you through. So do not be in a hurry. It will come. It is your privilege to say no to some expectations so that you can say yes to healing.

CHAPTER 6:

Goodness and Mercy

Surely goodness and mercy shall follow me
All the days of my life;
And I will dwell in the house of the Lord
Forever (Psalm 23:6).

I'm Being Followed

Journal Entry: How could it be that after all the crazy paths I've traveled, I am now so aware of it? I couldn't always tell what was going on because my focus was on just putting one foot in front of the other. But now I can see it. I can feel their presence with me and recognize how familiar they have become. The reality is I've been chased down and overtaken by my faithful companions. These two have been with me every step of the way from the first gasping tear until now. I feel as if I am exiting a harsh landscape and moving into the new horizons ahead. But I am not alone. I am being followed and joyfully chased into the sunshine of the Shepherd's love. (See Proverbs 4:18.)

Who is it that follows us? You need to know, my friend, because they are chasing you right now. Goodness and mercy are following

88 | HEALING JOURNEYS WITH THE *Shepherd*

us everywhere we go. And not just any goodness and mercy, but the pure, affectionate character of the living God. In the beginning, I told you about the Good Shepherd, and we reviewed the meaning of the word good: noble, wholesome, good-intentioned, and beautiful. You see, God is not just about *being* good. He is all about *doing* good. His deeply loving nature is equipped for action with a bountiful propensity to will and to do what is good, producing long-lasting benefits that flow from his own virtue. It is his determination to do good in your life if you will let him.

Let's take a minute to look back over your journey and remember where goodness showed up. Think about the last few months or years of your trek through healing. Can you see any goodness encounters? I remember so many:

- the search-and-rescue team from St. John's College in Santa Fe who sheltered us while they worked tirelessly in a storm to rescue my sons and recover my husband;
- the lady at the Social Security office who saw my grief and, in compassion, ushered me past the long line and straight into her office;
- the man who took my outdoor-loving son deer hunting;
- my nieces who thoughtfully sent just the right book of short encouragements;
- moments of worship when the warmth of God's presence surrounded me;
- long nights endured;
- new sunrises embraced;
- problems solved;
- provision given; and
- broken hearts restored over and over again.

Remembering these moments helps strengthen our hearts and reminds us how far we have come. You might want to take some time to journal about this. Make a goodness list of any big or small moments you can remember.

Our other constant traveling companion is mercy. Mercy and goodness are best friends, absolutely inseparable. Like goodness, mercy is an awe-inspiring aspect of God's character, unfailing love and tender-hearted kindness that goes on and on. Mercy is not a passive emotion but an active desire to remove the cause of distress from others. Mercy follows us through the valley experience. This is because the motivating force of God's heart is to heal us through and through, not just relieving our pain but removing what causes our greater brokenness. And in the process, he wins our hearts because mercy received produces in us grateful affection.

You delight in mercy.

I have to admit that at times, I have been too proud to accept his mercy. I was determined to stand on my own two feet and handle life my own way. But this pride opposed the mercy of God, causing me to slam the door of my heart and stop the flow of trust between us. Even so, I found that God is not stingy with his mercy and waited patiently for me to humble myself again and open the door. Then with eager delight, he rushed in with new mercies for a new morning. My willingness to receive his mercy always increases my ability to love him and love others. How sweet it is to know that God delights in showing us mercy.

Think with me for a moment. What do you look like fully standing in goodness and mercy? What does your loved one on the other side look like? You are both being followed by these faithful friends—you here on earth and your dear one in heaven. What an awesome thought. Even now, you have this experience of God's character in common. Let's consider what that looks like.

First of all, in spending time with the Shepherd, perhaps you experienced the deep affection of the Lord. You learned to glimpse the true beauty of your design, beginning to understand how you are known in heaven. Then there is the fragrance of love you carry, a unique blend of sweet perfume and smoke. You have been through the fire, and you smell like smoke. And yet the fragrance of Christ permeates every part of you, creating an irresistible aroma. You are more convinced of God's goodness than ever before, knowing firsthand the depths of your own weakness compared with the glorious heights of your strength when his unfailing love lifts you up.

Finally, a wonderful word describes our shining appearance: *shalom*.[15] I love this word, the Hebrew word for wholeness. It includes blessings of lasting peace, healing inside and out, restoration, fullness, completeness, well-being, and living in God's smile. Don't you love it? Now think about your loved one again. Even though you will always miss them on this side of life, can you picture them now, living in the shalom of God? No matter what they went through in the transition, all is well—for them and for you also. You continue your journey daily, growing in wholeness as the Good Shepherd leads you on past the valley.

---

15 *Blue Letter Bible* , "Lexicon :: Strong's H7965 – shalowm," June 13, 2019, https://www.blueletterbible.org/lang/lexicon/lexicon.cfm?t=kjv&strongs=h7965.

TAKE IT OR LEAVE IT

We have been through so much on this journey. The courage and tenderness we display are extraordinary. We walked by restful streams and rivers of tears. Father God covered us lovingly while we wrestled with hard questions and got to know his character more deeply than ever before. Dining at the table with a warrior king was one of my favorite moments of this quest. We gained strength as we lifted our sword to defeat enemies of doubt, loneliness, and fear. We found valuable treasure in unexpected places, adding a richness to our understanding of our eternal life span. Now, with new landscapes before us, we feel the strength of our hope returning.

I have good news for you. You made it through this journey of the valley of the shadow. You know by now that the experience is a living, organic one that cannot be rushed. You will experience more restoration as the Shepherd takes you into your new land. Writing this book for you twenty-plus years after my valley experiences has provided more time for my healing with the Shepherd. I am in awe of his continued care in my life. The wonder I feel in his presence never ends. I told you in the beginning that your job is to position yourself for healing at every turn. We still hold that posture as we exit this part of the valley. What a glorious life with new revelations of the deep love of God and greater skill to grow in our relationship with him.

Take some time to consider what to leave behind in the valley and what to take moving forward. I encourage you to make a list to help you remember and strengthen your resolve when the distractions of life happen. I encourage you to leave the following:

- What were the questions and doubts you resolved about yourself and God in "Paths Made Right?"

- Are there old belief systems you need to leave behind?
- Did you address bitterness, hurt feelings, or unforgiveness? Write these down.
- Even now, as you read this, you might be aware of someone you need to release and forgive. Go ahead, if you can, write it down even if it means determining to work on the issue as you move forward. Believe me, you do not want to take any extra people in your suitcase. You have wonderful things ahead of you. You don't want any unnecessary heaviness to hold you back.

Repacking your bag during a long trip feels great. Cleaning out the wadded-up, dirty clothes and throwing away trash makes more room for gifts and the new items you found on your journey. Remember the table the Shepherd set for you in the midst of your enemies? You faced some giants there: fear, despair, trauma, sorrow, self-pity, sickness, and unhealthy comforts. Write these down as a declaration of independence. The Shepherd defeated your enemies in his death and resurrection. He will continue to show you daily how to walk in more freedom. You do not have to be perfectly successful, but I think you will find great joy while you experience new ongoing freedom. Remember, goodness and mercy are following you everywhere.

I will forgive.

I want to note right here that you are not leaving your loved one behind. Yes, you heard me right. You worked hard to learn to say goodbye to them little by little. Those goodbyes to the life you once had together are precious and important. But you get to take all the best things your loved one brought to your life along with you. What did you learn from them? Did you learn about love? What valuable memories will you never forget? Take them with you in your journey. Those are precious gifts from your heavenly Father to hold on to. The truth is that they have now run ahead of you. Determine to make them proud with a life well lived, knowing that one day, you will each share new stories with perfect clarity and eternal perspective.

Now consider what else you want to take with you. Begin a new list of what you found in the valley to pack and carry on your journey. What did you learn about how your spirit, soul, and body are restored? What worked for you that you want to incorporate into your daily lifestyle? How did your prayer life change? Did you hear the voice of the Shepherd? Did you learn new ways to talk to God that you want to grow in? Look back at the list of blessings in the valley. What exchanges did you make? Write down the blessings you want to pack for the road ahead. Remember to grab a delectable snack from the table the Shepherd set for you.

It is time—time for you to enjoy the fruits of your labor and feed on his faithfulness. Because of God's grace-filled love, we can leave the past behind and take the most important things with us:

- the experience of the love of Jesus tried and true;
- a clean heart;
- strength you never knew you had;
- the best memories of your loved one;
- permission to live;
- new fighting skills;
- new concepts of heaven; and
- a confident hopeful expectation of God's goodness on future journeys.

These are worth the hard lessons you fought through to obtain them. Run into the sunshine with the Shepherd. Life really can be amazing again!

MORE THAN I COULD ASK OR IMAGINE

Journal Entry: The sounds of busy feet fill my house today. There are sweet baby giggles in the bedroom, and I have crayons in my coffee drawer. The boys are here with their families, and I feel as if my heart is about to burst! So many precious ones have been added to our story: beautiful and strong young women, the wives of my sons. They are my heroes. And I am so grateful for their love and steadying presence in a clan of wild, Scottish warriors. These—my children—are men and women of noble heart and fire-tested faith, each with their own unique and precious journey. "I have no greater joy than to know that they are walking in the truth with the Shepherd." (See 3 John 1:4.)

"All your children shall be taught by the Lord,
And great shall be the peace of your children"
(Isaiah 54:13).

What a crazy, wonderful journey! Now we know how to follow the Shepherd through hills and valleys, muck and mire, the highest joy, and the deepest sadness. The journey continues. Yes, it is very messy and so real. We learn anew every day the character of Father God as the Shepherd teaches us from the deep stores of his own pierced heart. His goodness is a greater reality than we could have ever imagined. The testing of his character in our eyes has proven that his intentions toward us are trustworthy and right and loving. He does not use his children for his own vague purposes. Nor does he make us suffer just to teach us a lesson. He truly is a good Father who delights in our journeys by pouring out mercy over and over again.

Now I see that this was a team effort. Before the foundations of the world were created, the Father, the Son, and Holy Spirit knew how my journey would unfold. How amazing! They planned and provided everything I would need to victoriously make it through the valley of the shadow, joyfully whole. And to top it all off, God gave me the gift of love again in my precious husband, Doug, who loves me so well and treasures all the journeys of my life. Truly I can say that goodness and mercy are following me all the days of my life. And the Shepherd? He loves me. Yes! He really, really loves me!

"Now to Him who is able to do exceedingly abundantly above all that we ask or think, according to the power that works in us, to Him be glory in the church by Christ Jesus to all generations, forever and ever. Amen" (Ephesians 3:20–21).

HEALING JOURNEYS WITH THE SHEPHERD:

40-Day Devotional

This daily devotional is written as a resource for those in grief recovery. It is based on my own journals and memories of my journeys. The personal entries included in this book are shared in hopes that you will identify with them through each of your shaky, brokenhearted steps and be comforted. I am choosing to write these in their raw and real state because to be honest, you just cannot fix this place. The only way is through. So take it one day at a time. Read each devotional as you can in any order you choose. There is no rush. Some days you will be able to do quite a bit. Other days, you might not read at all. It is okay. You are free to move at your own pace. You are never really alone on this journey. And you will find that this place is fertile ground for abundant grace and miracles as the Shepherd leads you through the valley of the shadow. As we travel together, I want you to know this one thing: You will make it. You really will. Resurrection life is waiting on the other side of the pain. And you can trust Jesus every day. He is the most gentle, the most loving, and the most powerful Shepherd. He is completely committed to you on your journey with him. His love for you is as deep and wide as the new landscape you face, and his love never fails.

My Shepherd

The Lord is my shepherd
I shall not want (Psalm 23:1).

My First Love

Journal Entry

"I was your first love, and I always will be." I remember these words as if they were engraved into my soul. This is my promise from my Shepherd, Jesus. In this, I feel his commitment to me. I will hold on to the promise, Lord. You are faithful. I will hold on to your love, no matter what. This is my vow to you.

Oh, Jesus, I don't know where we are going. What do I do now? I can't begin to wrap my head around all that is happening. It seems like a dream. Some moments, I have a little clarity. Other moments, my brain is so foggy, I can barely remember my own name. But here I am ... it's not a dream. And the only man I have ever loved is gone. Oh, my numb heart. Jesus, I love you. Will you show me how to walk this journey with you? I'm brokenhearted, but I do trust in your love for me. I'm so glad you are here with me. You are my first love, and you gave my husband to me. What a gift. Now he's with you ... and I'm with you ... and love continues. Whatever happens on this journey, Lord, I will not forget my first loves. I will not forget.

Practical Matters

The most important thing to remember as you begin your journey is that *you are loved*. The one who loves you most has hidden you in his heart. And he is fully committed to see you through every wobbly step of this journey. It will not be easy, and there are no short cuts. But his love *is* big enough for all that is ahead of you. You will never be alone, so just lean into his lovingkindness.

Word Strength

"The Lord has appeared of old to me, saying:

"Yes, I have loved you with an everlasting love;

Therefore with lovingkindness I have drawn you" (Jeremiah 31:3).

Prayer

Dear Shepherd, I need you so desperately now. Thank you for loving me and committing yourself to my journey. I say *yes* to your love, Jesus. I choose even now to lean in close to your heart and rest. This is my hiding place as I travel with you through the valley. No matter what happens, I will hold on to your love. You are my first love, and you always will be.

The Shepherd's Voice

Journal Entry

Well, it's all done. All the travel and funeral preparations finished. Lots of love from family and friends. Every hug was like a drink of water. Services are over. Everyone's departed here, back to their lives. My life seems as if it's in slow motion. The house feels so very empty today … like my heart. It's too quiet now. I'm left with my own thoughts. Sometimes they spin around and around in my head. Sometimes I am so numb and stare out the window. I don't know for how long; time isn't the same anymore. I'm lost in a sea of motion and emotion that seem to have no direction. The waves hit me out of nowhere, and some of them take me under until I don't know if I'll catch a breath again. I wait …. The distant yet familiar voice of the Shepherd whispers, "Just breathe. You can breathe under water. Just breathe." I've never been in a place like this before. I've never felt such pain. But I am impressed with the realization that Jesus's voice is here. I recognize it. Thank you, Shepherd. Oh, how I need you. Keep speaking, and I will try to hear you.

Practical Matters

Rest as much as possible. Do not fear the silence, for there you will hear the Shepherd's voice speak life to your heart. He knows how to speak to you in ways you can understand—even here. Ask him to help you in times when you strain to listen for any sound that might be him. In this strange and unfamiliar landscape, you might hear strange voices—voices of despair, fear, hopelessness, even death. Do not listen or entertain them, and they will fade away. Press into the arms of Jesus and listen to him instead. His voice, audible yet quiet, will soothe your soul as he begins to lead you forward.

Word Strength

"But he who enters by the door is the shepherd of the sheep. To him the doorkeeper opens, and the sheep hear his voice; and he calls his own sheep by name and leads them out. And when he brings out his own sheep, he goes before them; and the sheep follow him, for they know his voice. Yet they will by no means follow a stranger, but will flee from him, for they do not know the voice of strangers" (John 10:2–5).

Prayer

Jesus, you are my Shepherd, and I want to hear your voice, but you know my head feels a bit fuzzy right now. I ask you to speak to me through the noise of my life. I want to hear you above my own thoughts and cries. I want to hear you above the voices of others. Tune the ears of my heart to the frequencies of your voice. I will follow if I can hear you. So speak, Lord, I am listening.

Last Conversations – Socks

Journal Entry

"Mom, I can't find any socks." "Here are the only ones I can find, but they don't match," I replied, handing my son a laundry basket. "I'll get you some new ones before school starts."

"That's okay," my husband shouted from the bedroom. "We don't need matching socks to go camping. Come on, boys! Hurry up! We have to go now." And that was it. A goofy conversation about socks, a quick hug and kiss, and they were off.

Looking back, I can't believe that was our last conversation. Socks. Seriously? I wish we would have known. No, I don't. Yes, I do. No, I don't. At least, I wish we would have talked about something deep, like the meaning of life or something. Socks. As hard as I try to make that subject meaningful, I can't do it, except to think that we were just living life. I am happy about that. Of course, I thought I would see him again, and we would have a lot more time for deep conversations. But that's it. For now, anyway.

Practical Matters

What was your last conversation with your loved one? Most of us think about that conversation after they are gone and usually wish that we would have said something important. Well, I want to suggest that it is not too late. At times, you will feel the need to talk to the one you miss. Find a point of contact, a special place or item that connects you to them. Often people spend time at the cemetery where they can say unspoken words. You might also consider writing a letter to express your heart. Say "I love you." Say "I'm sorry." Say "I forgive you." Tell them about your life since they left. What do you miss about their presence in your world? Talk things over. Do they hear you? I do not know for sure, but I like to think they somehow do. The important part is that you need to say it. You need to share the unspoken words of your heart to them in a way that is real to you. And when those times to speak come, you will find deeper healing, resolution, and peace.

Word Strength

"Let the words of my mouth and the meditations of my heart be acceptable in Your sight, oh Lord, my strength and my redeemer" (Psalm 19:14).

Prayer

Jesus, I pray that you would bring to remembrance sweet, meaningful, and even funny words that have been spoken. Stir in me whatever words need to be shared to make further peace with one I am missing today. Lead me in your perfect timing as I courageously follow your steps. Give clarity of heart and thoughts as you help me form the words that express what I feel. Let life flow into the depths of my soul, releasing expressions of truth and love. Help me to say goodbye as I need to.

The Dove

Journal Entry

I went for walks every day after my dad passed away. I walked down our street and cried and breathed and remembered. One day, I heard a noise behind me, the coo of a bird. I turned around to see a little dove on the sidewalk. I enjoy doves so much—the funny way they walk with their heads bobbing and the sweet noises they make. I walked a little farther and felt the presence of someone watching me. Turning to look, I saw that it was the little dove, still with me!

So I asked him, "What are you doing here?" Immediately, I felt a comfortable peace engage my heart. I knew God was in this. I also remembered how much my father loved animals, especially turtle doves. I knew Daddy was in this moment too. So I looked at the little dove and said, "Daddy, is that you?" Now I don't believe in reincarnation. But I was trying to sort out the experience. My conclusion? That dove was there to comfort me. It was a gift from God who knew exactly what I needed. A simple little thing that represented a part of my relationship with my dad. Was dad in that plan? I think he was. And he delighted in the partnership with my heavenly Father and Holy Spirit to bring joy to my heart. And you know what? That little bird followed me every day on my walks for many days. I will always remember that gift of comfort from my two Daddies.

Practical Matters

Many of us find symbols of wonder that comfort us in our grief. Whether clearly from God or gifts from within our own soul, these can create meaningful moments of connection to the Shepherd and to the one we miss. My advice is do not overanalyze these experiences and keep Jesus in the center of all things. If the symbolic connection brings comfort and draws you closer to the Lord, receive it as a gift on the journey. One word of caution: resist any temptation to directly communicate with your loved one. Jesus is taking care of them in heaven, and he is taking care of you on earth. That is enough for now. Remember, a beautiful reunion is in your future.

Word Strength

"For the Lord will comfort Zion,
He will comfort all her waste places;
He will make her wilderness like Eden,
And her desert like the garden of the Lord;
Joy and gladness will be found in it,
Thanksgiving and the voice of melody" (Isaiah 51:3).

Prayer

Lord, my heart is looking for signs—signs of your presence, signs of comfort. I seem to be sensitive to these lately. I keep my eyes on you as you speak to me through calming and beautiful experiences. I receive your gifts in simple ways. Amen.

Where Am I?

Journal Entry

Where am I? What is this place? It's strange and dark, completely unrecognizable. I feel painfully alone, and yet I sense the presence of someone else. Who's there? I'm searching in the darkness for someone. Who's there? Can you help me? Can you explain to me what is happening? I can't see clearly. I feel as if I am looking through a gray fog. Everything is hazy in my heart and mind, and a weight of sadness is sitting on my chest. It hurts so much, like nothing I've ever felt before. The deep, deep moan of my soul is deafening to me. I want to run, to hide—anything to get away from it. Oh, Shepherd! What is this place? Please find me and take me away from here. Please—anywhere, anywhere but here. Can we leave now?

I used to be able to think positively and talk to myself on hard days. "Calm down. You're okay; just breathe and trust. Tomorrow will be a new day; tomorrow will be better." But tomorrow won't be better. I wake up every day and my first thought is, *"Oh, God. I'm still here in this pain. I thought it was a dream. But it's real. Tomorrow won't be better. It will take a long, long time to get to better days. I sense someone nearby, but I can't see them. Are you there? Please talk to me. Is it you, Jesus? Billy? Dad? Who's there? I know someone is here. Where are you?*

Suddenly, a momentary break in my despair—a breath of wind—blows across my soul. It's Jesus. I know because I have felt this peace before but never with this depth. It's comforting. But a power in it is new to me ... like a passionate determination ... a jealous fury on my behalf. It's hard to explain. But I know in an instant a new dimension of my Shepherd. He sees me in this moment of pain: my bruised heart, my weak faith, and my weary mind. He knows I am here, lying wounded in this crag of the cliff on the edge of the valley. I see my Shepherd-Warrior, guarding me with great zeal. He lifts my head to offer me a drink. I feel a little refreshed. I still have no energy for words, but as I look up into his loving gaze, we exchange a deep affection. "I trust you, Shepherd."

"I know," he replies.

Practical Matters

Take it easy. I know these days can feel very lonely and disorienting. But take it easy. It will not last forever. Better days are coming. What should you do in the meantime? Just breathe until you are alive again, until the fog begins to clear and your strength returns. Let the Shepherd hide you in the cleft of the rock where you can rest and heal, the place of glory revealed even if you cannot see it today. He is there with you.

Word Strength

"So it shall be, while My glory passes by, that I will put you in the cleft of the rock, and will cover you with My hand while I pass by" (Exodus 33:22).

Prayer

Jesus, I need you. Please show me your presence. I feel weary and sad. Come closer, Shepherd. Hide me away in you until I can lift my head again. I want to see your glory passing by, but I do not have the strength to perceive it now. So I will wait here in the quiet, knowing you care for me. I love you, Jesus. I trust you.

Cleaning Out Closets

Journal Entry

His clothes—his jeans, T-shirts, the colorful cowboy shirts he loved to wear—were still in my closet after six months. Some days, I ignored them completely, only looking at my side of the closet. Other times, with trembling hands, I reached out and ran my fingers along the soft fabric or moved my face close to see if I could still smell him there. But something new happened today. I suddenly had the urge to put his things away. I don't know why. I just did. So I got some boxes, folded the clothes neatly, and packed them away. I stood in the closet, looking at the empty space. I thought I would feel a lot of pain, but I didn't. It felt mostly okay, as if it were the right thing at the right time. I want to be sure and keep certain things for the boys. I have no idea what they will need or want, but I'll do my best.

Practical Matters

Knowing what to do with your loved one's personal items can overwhelm you. Packing, selling, or throwing them away is a daunting task. But I believe it is an important part of the healing process. There are no time limits here. You do not have to rush. You can trust yourself to know when the time is right to start cleaning. And you will most likely do it in stages. If you are holding on to items, and you feel sad or stuck, you might consider taking action. If you have someone to help you, invite them over and take on what you can. You might need to do some sorting alone so that you can sort your heart as well. Store anything you think you might want in years to come. Take photos of items you do not want to keep but want to remember. Shadow boxes are a great way to display small mementos.

Word Strength

"Therefore, if anyone is in Christ, he is a new creation; old things have passed away; behold, all things have become new" (2 Corinthians 5:17).

Prayer

Lord, I want to thank you for all the memories left behind from the life of the one I care about. Help me to let go little by little. Comfort my heart as I remember and release. Watch over me as I work, and show me what is important to keep for the future. I lean into your love today, my Shepherd. Amen.

The Gift of Time

Journal Entry

Someone told me today, "You have all the time in the world. Time heals all wounds." It sounded helpful at the time, but now I'm not sure what to think about it. How long will it take to heal this broken heart? Six months? A year or a hundred? I'm not sure time is on my side here. I hope there is more to this than I can see now. When I settle in with the Shepherd, I am at ease with permission to live in my own timing. I don't know if that's right or if that's what everyone else does in loss. But I know in my heart, it's all I can do. And it is the right thing for me.

Practical Matters

If there is one word of encouragement I can give you here, it is this: Take your time. Do not rush through this process. I know how badly you just want the pain to be over so that your heart can beat normally again. Time seems to be your enemy and not your friend. In moments or seasons of deep pain, when it feels as if time is against us, we need someone who is not bound by the limitations of time to actively restore our past, present, and future. God is who was and who is and who is to come. He lives in an eternal time frame, not a natural one. And he can bridge all the gaps in your history into one glorious story of redemption.

Word Strength

"To everything there is a season,
A time for every purpose under heaven:
A time to be born,
And a time to die;
A time to plant,

And a time to pluck what is planted;
A time to kill,
And a time to heal;
A time to break down,
And a time to build up;
A time to weep,
And a time to laugh;
A time to mourn,
And a time to dance" (Ecclesiastes 3:1–4).

Prayer

Jesus, you are the Lord of time. And you are the Lord of my season of healing. You know my story from beginning to end, making everything beautiful in its time. So, Lord, help me to take my time to heal completely. I want to do all you have in mind for me. If my times are in your hands, I have all the time I need. Amen.

Decisions, Decisions

Journal Entry

Why do people have to make so many decisions when someone dies? It is the worst possible time to try to think about anything clearly. Finances, housing, kids, school, work—I can't even decide what clothes to wear today. I have some support, but I feel very alone in these big decisions. What if I make the wrong choice? The last thing we need is more trouble because I didn't know what to do. The Shepherd reminds me to settle down and take one day at a time. All I have to do is trust him and just do today.

Practical Matters

It is crazy how bereaved husbands, wives, sons, daughters, parents, and friends have to make big decisions when they are clearly not at their best. But you are not alone, my friend. Try to focus on one thing at a time. Ask for help. Ask for more time to make your decision. Have someone you trust gather information for you. Take your concern to the Lord and let him guide you. He really will. There are good answers but no perfect ones. You are free to do your best with the information you have right now. You are also free to make mistakes. The Lord will help you get back on track if you do. He is so very trustworthy. You can rely on his wise heart during this time.

Word Strength

"Trust God from the bottom of your heart;
don't try to figure out everything on your own.
Listen for God's voice in everything you do, everywhere you go;

he's the one who will keep you on track" (Proverbs 3:5–6 MSG).

Prayer

Lord, you know all the things I am trying to think about today. But my mind is so foggy; my heart, numb. Please help me with these decisions. I bring them to you and ask for your wisdom to cut through my grief. Bring clarity, God. Help me be aware of those around me who can assist me. Show me who to trust. I trust you, my Shepherd. Amen.

My Soul Restored

He makes me to lie down in green pastures
He leads me beside the still waters
He restores my soul (Psalm 23:2–3).

My Place

Journal Entry

I love this place. My heart sighs in relief at the sound of the water and the wind moving gently through the leaves. They fill my senses with a renewed desire to engage and enjoy life. I can do life well if I live from the simple place, the place where beauty and peace flow around and through me, caressing my soul to gently lay down my burdens in the Shepherd's care. Here I can receive the quiet wisdom not available in my own preoccupied mind. And with it comes strong resolve, bubbling up like a natural spring with a constant flow of refreshing understanding. The how and why of my life blend into the movement of Holy Spirit with my spirit, and I know all is well. All is well.

Practical Matters

Take time to find your place. Everyone needs a special place to reconnect with their own heart, a place where inspiration and comfort flow. A place just for you. It might be as simple as the comfortable, overstuffed chair in your bedroom. It might be a bench at the park or a walking path in the country. As you heal, look for your place. Then go there often. Quiet your soul. Listen. Feel. Receive. Do not forget in the midst of your busy, stressful days to spend minutes or hours in your place. You will be glad you did.

Word Strength

"'Everyone who thirsts, come to the waters;
And you who have no money come, buy grain and eat.
Come, buy wine and milk

Without money and without cost [simply accept it as a gift from God].

Why do you spend money for that which is not bread,

And your earnings for what does not satisfy?

Listen carefully to Me, and eat what is good,

And let your soul delight in abundance'" (Isaiah 55:1–2).

Prayer

Kind Shepherd, I hear your invitation to come and let my soul delight in your abundance. I long for the place where I do not have to stress and worry about how to afford or obtain what I need. Help me find my place. Help me learn to be still and enjoy all you provide for me as I slow down into the unforced rhythms of grace in the flow of your goodness. Amen.

Sunshine

Journal Entry

Every morning, I sit in the sunshine and let its warmth comfort me. It's cold outside today, so I found a spot where the sun was shining through my front window onto the floor. I feel the presence of God. The light on my face reminds me that he is near. I connect with him and let the warmth envelope me. I love this place. I'll be back here tomorrow.

Practical Matters

Simple comforts are important during these days. Allow yourself time to soak up some sunshine even if it's only a few minutes. It will do your mind and body good. You likely need increased amounts of Vitamin D. The sun will help. You might also want to talk to your health professional about a supplement. A boost of D can improve your mood as well. Let this moment in the sun be a time to receive the warmth and the light that you so desperately need. Slow your thinking. Get in touch with your spirit and let the Spirit of God wrap you in grace.

Word Strength

"His splendor and majesty covers the heavens
And the earth is full of His praise.
His brightness is like the sunlight;
He has [bright] rays flashing from His hand,
And there [in the sunlike splendor] is the hiding place of His power" (Habakkuk 3:3–4 AMP).

Prayer

Lord, I thank you for the light of your grace surrounding me today. I rest in the warmth of your light as it brings comfort and connection with your presence, your power, and your grace.

Sleep

Journal Entry

It's been a few months now, and I am still so tired. I think I'm more tired now than I was during the first days of the journey. It's a different kind of tired. My body feels old and achy. My joints throb, and my neck and shoulders are killing me. I can't seem to remember things, simple things. I was talking with a group of friends the other day. One of them asked me an easy question, and I drew a complete blank. I felt so dumb. I stared at them and couldn't answer. After an awkward moment, they graciously let it go and continued their conversation. As I write this, I realize that I am not getting much sleep. I can go to sleep when I first go to bed. It's a welcome relief. But I wake up after a couple of hours and can't fall back asleep. I don't even know the last time I had a good night's sleep.

Practical Matters

Sleep is absolutely essential. We don't always realize how little we are sleeping, especially in high-stress seasons. You need eight to nine hours per night if possible. You honestly do. Your body needs that much to properly renew itself. You might need even more than that during this hard journey. Naps are okay. Consider keeping a calendar or journal or using an app to track your sleep. You might not know how you're really doing. Be sure that you establish a slowdown ritual at the end of the day to prepare for sleep. Reduce noise, light, and activity. Light a candle, or take a bath. Avoid screen time two hours before bed. The light triggers your brain to stay awake. Limit alcohol. It might relax you so that you fall asleep. But the sugar content is a stimulant and will wake you back up in two or three hours. As you lie down, take five deep breaths, exhaling slowly. If you need more help, contact your health professional for recommendations of supplements or additional support.

Word Strength

"I will both lie down in peace, and sleep;
For You alone, O Lord, make me dwell in safety" (Psalm 4:8).

Prayer

Lord, I ask you to bring deep peace to my mind tonight. Let your restful love fill every thought, every breath. Restore my body and soul with sweet sleep. Comfort my troubled mind and bring relief from anxious ramblings. Let me feel your presence as you sweep over me with deep peace. Breathe ... Breathe ... Falling ... Falling into sleep ...

Just Make the Bed

Journal Entry

It seems like forever since I had the energy to accomplish much. I wish I felt like doing something, but I just don't. It feels as if I have weights attached to my body. I should be busy. After all, it's been a few months, but I barely seem to make it through the day. Now I understand what my mother used to say after my dad died. "Some days, all I can do is make the bed." So true. So I guess I'll just try to make my bed and view that as an accomplishment. Of course, that means I have to get out of it first. Hmmm.

Practical Matters

It is normal to have little energy for a long time after a loss. Be patient with yourself. That energy is not just draining out the bottom of your feet. It is going to help you heal from the inside out, so you are accomplishing more than you know. Set simple, achievable goals for yourself at home and at work. Do one thing at a time. Manage chores as you can. Tackle a small pile of paperwork. If you are working full-time at a stressful position, give yourself permission to ask for help with the house. Go ahead. Pay someone else to make your bed. Or have a friend do a chore for you here and there. It does not make you weak but smart. You will regain your energy in time but accept the fact that it will take a while.

Word Strength

"Strengthen the weak hands,
And make firm the feeble knees.
Say to those who are fearful-hearted,
'Be strong, do not fear!
Behold, your God will come with vengeance,

With the recompense of God;
He will come and save you.'
Then the eyes of the blind shall be opened,
And the ears of the deaf shall be unstopped.
Then the lame shall leap like a deer,
And the tongue of the dumb sing.
For waters shall burst forth in the wilderness,
And streams in the desert." (Isaiah 35:3–6).

Prayer

Lord, I want to be strong, but I feel so weak. Would you help me? Help me to not only be strong but to be weak. Give me the presence of mind to ask for help where I can. Strengthen my weak hands day by day. Come and save me from my fears. I ask for your strength to flow like streams in the desert, filling every dry and empty crevasse with your mighty grace.

A Walk

Journal Entry

Today I went for a walk around the lake and up to the chapel. It felt good to get up and out of the house. I started out slowly but gained new energy with each step. I can go farther now than I used to. I talked as I walked—to myself, to the one I miss, and to God. I wonder if my neighbors see me and wonder who I'm talking to. But I don't care. It helps me so much. Every day, I feel strength building in me and fear and anxiety leave as I start my walk. I've been singing a little song to the beat of my steps that helps me on my journey.

Practical Matters

Go for a walk every day if possible. Do what you have energy for, even if it is just to walk down your block and back or for a moment during your lunch hour. Get outside. Move your body. Stretch out your five senses. As you move, notice everything around you. See the sunlight through the trees. Listen to the birds chirping, dogs barking, and children playing. Smell the fresh air. And feel the wind on your cheeks. Let your heart stretch a little too. Even a short walk will bring new energy to your body and soul. You might be able to walk in your neighborhood or at a nearby park. As you gain strength, venture to other places of interest, such as a hiking path or trail in a different area.

Walk with a friend. Share your journey with a close confidant. Stop and pray together. Walk alone as well. During daily times alone, I could lean fully into God's comfort and direction. Walking by myself allowed me time to listen to God, to my own heart, and to my body. The movement of my feet carrying me down the pathways helped me to open up and release the physical and emotional stress I was holding. During these times of honest movement, I sometimes gained new insight to a practical challenge or broke through a stuck place of anger or fear. We need time alone to process well and learn to be okay with ourselves.

Word Strength

"I will walk before the Lord
In the land of the living." (Psalm 116:9).

"Cause me to hear Your lovingkindness in the morning,
For in You do I trust;
Cause me to know the way in which I should walk,
For I lift up my soul to You." (Psalm 143:8).

Prayer

Thank you, God, for life today. I get to walk in the land of the living, and yet you see my heart. You know how much I miss my loved one. I trust you, God, to lead me in every step as you guide me through my healing journey. One step at a time, one foot in front of the other, I will walk, for you, my Shepherd, are right by my side.

Green Pastures

Journal Entry

I finally got outside to be with the Lord. I found a sweet spot on the steps by the rose garden. The grass is so lush and green, the kind of bright, alive green that just makes me happy. It is hard for me to stay still for very long. My mind races and runs through lists and elusive endless rabbit trails that lead me nowhere. As I focus on Psalm 23 once again, I watch the squirrels play in the lawn as the deer come to graze and rest. To them, the green grass means nourishment, essential food, and water. For me, it refreshes my soul, reminding me that life goes on, season by season, renewed over and over again. My life is the same. Season by season, I am renewed in the loving care of the Shepherd. He walks me daily to the green pasture where I can rest. I sit in the tender shoots of grass, absorbing his nourishment. No matter where life's seasons find me, I know spring will come again. His Word is true, and he loves me still.

Practical Matters

Look for life around you. Physically engage with nature when you can. Take your shoes off and stand in the cool grass. Use your senses to experience life in small ways. Sit with the Shepherd in loving silence, and let him nourish your heart with his presence. Remember, this is one season of many in your life. Spring will come again, and life will renew itself because that is what life does. It is a powerful force. Jesus is the resurrection and the life, and he is working in you today.

Word Strength

"He makes me to lie down in green pastures;

He leads me beside the still waters" (Psalm 23:2).

Prayer

Lord, I am here. I will lie down in your green pastures today. I will be still and rest and let you restore my soul. Jesus, you are the one who loves me most. Slow me down. Show me how to do this. You know it is not easy for me to be still. But I want to be. I need to be. I will be still. Infuse me again with life that comes from your heart. I pray that I would feel your goodness as I draw nourishment from your love.

Dancing with the Shepherd

Journal Entry

Yesterday I received a card from my friend Sue. She shared words of comfort and prayer and then closed by saying, "It's okay to dance." Dance? This word stirred inside me. I awoke this morning with a little energy. I feel a need to move a bit more. I also sense an invitation from the Lord. "Come and dance with me." Well, I know how to waltz and two-step, so maybe I'll give it a try. What do I have to lose? The kids are at school, and I have the house to myself.

I put on my favorite worship music and focused on what the Shepherd was doing in my heart. At first, I just swayed to the music. Then I lifted my arms and began to wave them too. I felt the loving embrace of the Shepherd and remembered dancing with my daddy as a little girl, standing on his feet as he stepped to the music. This is a sweet place. The movement feels good to my weary body, and my heart seems to be opening up. I'll think I'll dance again tomorrow ...

Practical Matters

Dancing can be a wonderful healing expression of movement. Find a place where no one can see you: your living room, bedroom, or patio. Put on some slow music you enjoy, something Christ-centered. Remember, the purpose of dance is worship. It helps me to have something like a scarf in my hand to wave. Just move slowly with the music as your heart opens up. Move as you feel comfortable. Before you know it, you will be swirling and spinning with the Shepherd in a healing, freeing experience.

Word Strength

"You have turned for me my mourning into dancing;

You have put off my sackcloth and clothed me with gladness,

To the end that my glory may sing praise to You and not be silent.

O Lord my God, I will give thanks to You forever" (Psalm 30:11–12).

Prayer

Thank you, Lord, for your invitation to dance. I feel the flow of your healing in my life and sense a swirl of brilliant glory filling spaces in my soul. I want more freedom to move with the colorful rhythms of your grace. Would you show me what that looks like for me? I am a little unsure. This is a new place for me, but I want to grow into it with you. I accept your invitation to dance in the loving embrace of your mercy. I will watch your feet intently as you teach me the dance for the season ahead. Amen.

Made Right Again

*He leads me in paths of righteousness
For His name's sake (Psalm 23:3).*

Realign

Journal Entry

God, where are you? Who are you? I thought I knew what I believed, but now everything seems to be turned upside down. I don't know anything anymore. I guess I thought that if we loved you and did our best, you would keep us safe and bad things wouldn't happen to us. I read my Word now and am challenged by it as I can't figure out how some of the promises I have clung to my whole life apply in the middle of this tragedy. Where do I go from here? I don't want to be angry and bitter. I've seen the sour faces of people whose stories turned into bitterness, their eyes empty because of the hardness of hope deferred, their joy stolen. They are heartsick and forever misaligned. I don't understand all this. Portions of the foundation of my faith are in ruins. But I refuse to give up. Somehow your love within me causes my heart to press forward, crying out, "This isn't all there is. There must be more than this." Shepherd, I will follow you, no matter what. It is the only choice my heart can make. So here I am again today. Teach me who you really are, not my second-grade Sunday School Jesus, but the Jesus who commands the storm in my heart and calls me beyond the tossing waves with powerful love I can trust. Realign my heart and mind to your truth. I must know you.

Practical Matters

During this journey, you will have many opportunities to realign what you thought you believed about God as you wrestle with your loss. Draw from the lessons you have already learned. But know there is more. God is bigger, more powerful, and more loving than you ever dreamed possible. The paradigm shifts might feel uncomfortable. Be determined to keep your heart open, and the Lord will faithfully lead you as you grow in understanding. Prove what you think you know. In the end, values and beliefs of pure gold will remain, and you will be amazing and strong.

Word Strength

" ... and in the midst of the seven lampstands One like the Son of Man, clothed with a garment down to the feet and girded about the chest with a golden band. His head and hair were white like wool, as white as snow, and His eyes like a flame of fire; His feet were like fine brass, as if refined in a furnace, and His voice as the sound of many waters; He had in His right hand seven stars, out of His mouth went a sharp two-edged sword, and His countenance was like the sun shining in its strength." (Revelation 1:13–16).

Prayer

Lord Jesus, I want to know you—really know you. I am so comforted by the sweetness of your shepherding hands. But today, Lord, I need a warrior. I need to know you as my all-powerful, fiery, sovereign King. I choose to align myself with the truth of your Word as you change my perspective on life and faith. There must be more than I've known before. So here I am, God. Show me who you are in your strength. Command the storm in my heart and realign my understanding with your powerful goodness. Amen.

I'm Just so Mad

Journal Entry

Intensely broken, damaged, unable to breathe, gasping from the pain of grief, I continued to walk. Although the valley held beauty, it only fueled my anger. How could it be beautiful when my world had collapsed? How could anything ever be beautiful again? I didn't understand. I was too damaged to care. I cried out from the depths of me yet found nothing to console me. I desperately wandered in this valley, stumbling along the way. I cried from the brokenness, afraid of sinking into the darkness. "Help me, Lord, please help me. If you don't rescue me, I'll die, and I won't care. Help me, please, help me. However you can, however it appears, I stand before you, stripped of all. Please do something—anything—to relieve this pain." (Lynnette Watkins)

Practical Matters

Here is what I want to tell you: You will experience anger on your journey, which is a normal stage of grief. You might become fussy and snippy—your family will tell you!—or even want to scream, yell, and throw things. This is a painful transition into acceptance. The Bible tells us, "Be angry, and do not sin ... " (Ephesians 4:26). Anger is not bad. As a matter of fact, its energy propels you forward. But that does not mean you can be hurtful to yourself or others. Find real and safe ways to release your anger. I once bought a box of clay skeet targets and threw them off a cliff. They break easily and are biodegradable. Ha! Another time, I hit baseballs in the batting cages. Cry out to God. He is not afraid of or offended by your anger. Really! He knows you are angry anyway. Acknowledging how you truly feel keeps the doors of communication open and allows him to deeply comfort you.

Word Strength

"Be angry, and do not sin: do not let the sun go down on your wrath, nor give place to the devil" (Ephesians 4:26–27).

Prayer

Shepherd, I feel so hurt and awful. I am just so mad, and I do not know what to do with this jumble of emotions. Everything seems so wrong to me. I am sorry I feel this way. But you already know, don't you, God? Oh, come, Lord! You're not afraid or offended by my anger, so come. I invite you into every place of deep hurt and disappointment. Help me know how to release my anger in safe ways. Forgive me for anything I have said or done that has hurt those around me. Forgive me for anything I've done to hurt me. I surrender all this to you. Help me release and receive … release and receive …. Then compel me forward toward my next steps of healing. Amen.

Hope

Journal Entry

Today I went swimming with some friends in a fresh water spring. The cool water refreshed my tired body. But my soul deeply yearns for something more. I don't even know what it is. It mingles with the aching sighs of my parched heart. I wish the water could flood that space. I don't really want to go to church much anymore. I feel as if everyone looks at me with kindness but with pity. I don't want to answer questions. "How are you?" Now there's a good one for you. There's no way to answer that in this space. It would take me a year to tell you how I really am. So I just say, "Fine." Not even true. I wish my life was the way it used to be. I loved being in worship. It brought such joy to my heart. Where did that go? Where is that hope that used to be so vibrant within me? Why am I still so sad?

Practical Matters

Hope is the confident expectation of good. It takes a while to recover your hope after a loss. No matter your circumstance, the experience of death can zap the hope right from your soul. Again, the questions of God's goodness emerge at every turn. But recovery of hope is possible. Be patient with yourself. Point your attention to the love of God and keep moving forward. In Psalm 42, David talked to himself about his sorrow and was refreshed by his real conversation with God about his pain. Read this passage aloud and see new hope restored in the depths of your soul. Then write down the phrases that comfort you most.

Word Strength

"As the deer pants for the water brooks,

So pants my soul for You, O God.
My soul thirsts for God, for the living God.
When shall I come and appear before God?
My tears have been my food day and night,
While they continually say to me,
"Where is your God?"
When I remember these things,
I pour out my soul within me.
For I used to go with the multitude;
I went with them to the house of God,
With the voice of joy and praise,
With a multitude that kept a pilgrim feast.
Why are you cast down, O my soul?
And why are you disquieted within me?
Hope in God, for I shall yet praise Him
For the help of His countenance.
O my God, my soul is cast down within me;
Therefore I will remember You from the land of the Jordan,
And from the heights of Hermon,
From the Hill Mizar.
Deep calls unto deep at the noise of Your waterfalls;
All Your waves and billows have gone over me.
The Lord will command His lovingkindness in the daytime,
And in the night His song shall be with me—
A prayer to the God of my life" (Psalm 42:1–8).

Prayer

Lord, the deep in me is calling out to the deep in you. I am thirsty for more than tears I choose to hope in you. I choose to believe in your goodness as you restore my soul. I will put my hope in you. Amen.

Guard Your Heart

Journal Entry

Today, as I write, my heart stirs with sadness, questions, and even new ideas. Maybe if I move to a new city, all my problems will magically disappear, and I can start over with all this. I have this strange, new urge to run, to just get away from it all—every familiar sight, sound, and person. My heart seems a little wild, as if it wants to wander off somewhere. Where? I don't know, just anywhere but here. I spend a lot of time lately, daydreaming of new scenes of life in Hawaii, the mountains, etc. What is going on with you, restless heart? How are you? I hear the answer of my heart combined with the loving whispers of the Shepherd. My heart says, "I am tired and ready to do something else." The Shepherd says, "You are tired, and I am stirring new possibilities within you. But hold steady. It is not time yet. Beloved, stay with it. Stay steady."

Practical Matters

How is your heart today? Take a few minutes to ask yourself this question. Staying connected to your own heart is an important part of your care because what is inside comes out. And it is your job to manage it. Acknowledging the workings of the seat of your emotions, life, and passion is a way to show kindness to yourself. It can allow you to know what is there and guard it well, whether it is sadness, doubt, creative solutions, or new perspectives. Take a look daily. It might sound strange, but ask your heart how it is doing. Then be compassionate in your response. Ask God to fill every space in your heart with his peace, the shalom of God that brings healing and wholeness to your life step-by-step.

Word Strength

"Keep your heart with all diligence,
For out of it spring the issues of life" (Proverbs 4:23).

"Be anxious for nothing, but in everything by prayer and supplication, with thanksgiving, let your requests be made known to God; and the peace of God, which surpasses all understanding, will guard your hearts and minds through Christ Jesus" (Philippians 4:6–7).

Prayer

Lord, your Word says that I can tell you everything that is in my heart and that your peace will guard my heart and mind. So today I want to get in touch with my own heart. It is a little scary because so much is there. Show me anything I need to acknowledge and release to you. (Take time to listen.) I lift up what you are highlighting to me. (Specifically surrender the things he brings to mind to him.) I ask you for help in guarding these areas of my heart as I heal. Let your peace fill every space within me. I receive your healing peace now. Amen.

Going in Circles

Journal Entry

Today I feel as if I am going around in circles. I have days that seem better, and I think, *Okay, good! I'm moving forward. Now we're getting somewhere.* And then, smash! Another wave hits me, or something triggers my emotions all over again. I can go from zero to a hot mess in three seconds. I am learning that if I look for the Shepherd in these moments, I can see him clearly leading me to something important. It's like circling around a search area again to find what I've been missing. One more pass, but this time a little deeper, a little closer, a better view. I like to reach my goals in five easy steps. I have my well-planned list of the stages of grief. But goodness, gracious. I zigzag all over the place, sometimes all in one day. I guess this trip is more unpredictable than I expected. No one-two-three and we're done.

Practical Matters

Grief is not a linear process going straight from point A to point B. It is actually cyclical in most of its motion with circular windings around and around. It moves up and down, higher and deeper. It moves out wide and then pulls back in, closing the circle tight again. Are you dizzy? It can be challenging to know how to measure your progress. Did someone give you a hand out or book on the stages of grief? Read it as it can help you identify some of what you are experiencing. Just know it is not a straight path. But as we cooperate with the movement of each cycle, something powerful is happening. Space is being created in our soul. Ever-increasing in its width and depth, the capacity of our heart is becoming great. It is growing in its ability to hold and store the secrets of life and love and heaven.

Word Strength

"For this reason I bow my knees to the Father of our Lord Jesus Christ, from whom the whole family in heaven and earth is named, that He would grant you, according to the riches of His glory, to be strengthened with might through His Spirit in the inner man, that Christ may dwell in your hearts through faith; that you, being rooted and grounded in love, may be able to comprehend with all the saints what is the width and length and depth and height—to know the love of Christ which passes knowledge; that you may be filled with all the fullness of God" (Ephesians 3:14–19).

Prayer

Father in heaven, I ask that you strengthen me by your Spirit, deep on the inside. Increase my capacity to know how deep, how high, and how wide is your great love. And then fill me with all the fullness of you. Amen.

Write It Down

Journal Entry

Here I am again, thinking and feeling so many things. My head and heart are so full. I go round and round in my head, trying to understand, to figure things out. Why? Why did all this happen? What am I supposed to do now? How do I make all these decisions? How do I go on with so much pain inside? Will it ever go away? Will I feel better someday? So many questions and so many elusive answers. They constantly swirl within me day and night. How can I slow them down? I need to release some of the pressure in my head and my chest. I have this feeling that the answers do exist somewhere out there. Maybe it's just not time to know some things. I'm waiting. Shepherd, what should I do while I wait?

Practical Matters

Journaling is one of the most effective ways to sort out the deep feelings and questions of this journey. It truly is a relief to let the paper hold some of the weight of your burdens. In chapter one, I gave some detailed instructions about how to write these down. My favorite way is to buy a simple spiral notebook and write two to three pages a day. Just write whatever enters your mind, even if it does not make sense. Pour out some of the jumbled thoughts in your head onto the page. This is just for you, to help you sort out your insides. You do not have to be neat or happy or even nice. You want an honest flow of thoughts and emotions. It is like turning on a faucet that has not been used in a long time. It might take a little priming of the pump to get the water flowing, but if you write a little every day, it will come. Before you know it, deep thoughts and feelings will gush forth on the page. This is a safe place. And the Shepherd will help regulate the volume so that you can manage little by little. Healing conversations, helpful solutions, and relief from tears released will help you. Give it a try.

Word Strength

"I cry out to the Lord with my voice;
With my voice to the Lord I make my supplication.
I pour out my complaint before Him;
I declare before Him my trouble.

When my spirit was overwhelmed within me,
Then You knew my path.
In the way in which I walk
They have secretly set a snare for me" (Psalm 142:1–3).

Prayer

Lord, I know you hear the cry of my heart. You know every need, every ache, and every question that troubles me. Thank you for giving me freedom to pour out my complaint, to moan and cry, to sort and heal. Give me courage to be real and honest on the page, to let the flow happen. I invite you to walk with me as I write. Speak to my heart. Ease my mind. And lift the weight as I release some of what is in me.

My Lost Song

Journal Entry

In the midst of my grief, my anger, my hopelessness, I find a song—a symbol of hope, of life—a song well beyond myself. My Shepherd has led me to this place and given me that single tone. Whatever it looks like, however it sounds or feels, he knows what I need and how I can relate. He is the restorer Shepherd and the one who knows the way through this maze of grief. A single note beckoning, becoming, developing, blending, blossoming into more. Compelling me to listen, to join, to participate as it engaged my spirit and mind. As subtle as a flutter in the wind, still it drew me. A tone invited the soft, the loud, melody and harmony, then rhythm. It was given to radiance, radiance, a glow so closely related to the sound that only a frequency has to be altered to make the tone a beam of light—illumination of body, mind, and spirit. The sound, becoming the very breath of God. The song that can recreate life, heal, restore, and bring peace. He has led me to the rock and wrapped his arms around me. His wings embrace me, parting the feathers to reveal only what I need and give confidence to know I am not alone. Day by day, he sings over me; he holds me and loves on me. Day by day, I live. (Lynette Watkins)

Practical Matters

Take time to listen for sounds that soothe and heal. Your favorite songs might be a great start. But in your search for comfort, open up to new possibilities: a new instrumental album, a fresh worship song that makes your spirit sing, even the song of spring birds or the laughter of children. As you search for resonance in the tones of life, listen closely. Within the Shepherd's heart, your song is playing. Allow him to hold you in the shelter of his love and sing over you. There is no better place to be.

Word Strength

"The Lord your God in your midst,
The Mighty One, will save;
He will rejoice over you with gladness,
He will quiet you with His love,
He will rejoice over you with singing" (Zephaniah 3:17).

Prayer

Lord, I open the ears of my heart to you. Tune my being to your songs of love. I want to hear the sounds of heaven that bring me life and make me feel the comforting melodies, realigning my soul. Thank you for singing over me. Help me hear it. Help me feel it. Amen.

The Valley of the Shadow

Yea, though I walk through the valley of the shadow of death,
I will fear no evil;
For You are with me;
Your rod and Your staff, they comfort me.
You prepare a table before me in the presence of my
enemies (Psalm 23:4–5).

Holding onto the Rock

Journal Entry

Sobbing and afraid, I was transformed. I had unknowingly opened the door to peace. In the valley of the shadow of death, I found myself on a rock, a huge boulder worn smooth by tears. It was hollowed out like a cradle, retaining the warmth of the stippled sun through the leaves of a nearby tree. I lay there, soaking up the comfort, cradled in the lap of the Creator of the world, knowing somehow, I would breath again. I will survive. I will want to. I will. (Lynette Watkins)

Practical Matters

Throughout the valley journey, we have a daily choice: to live, to rest, to receive, to love, to just breathe. Sometimes you can just walk through this place of recovery one choice at a time, one day at a time. That is good news. Sometimes, you can just walk through the next thirty minutes. Try not to look too far ahead. Open the door to peace each day and then rest in the lap of your Creator. He is recreating you in his powerful love. He will take every weak yes you give him. It is the stuff of miracles.

Word Strength

"Hear my cry, O God;
Attend to my prayer.
From the end of the earth I will cry to You,
When my heart is overwhelmed;
Lead me to the rock that is higher than I.

For You have been a shelter for me,
A strong tower from the enemy.

I will abide in Your tabernacle forever;

I will trust in the shelter of Your wings. Selah" (Psalm 61:1–4).

Prayer

Lord, I open the door to peace. Cradled safe in your love, I believe you hear my cries and are responding in mercy. I find peace in your compassion. The warmth of your presence soothes my heart. The door is open, my Creator. Come in and rest here with me. I choose to breathe, to survive, to live. Amen.

Longing for Spring

Journal Entry

Good morning, Shepherd. It's cold again this morning. I am weary of the winter and ready for a fresh season. Energy is emerging inside me, bringing a desire to clean up things and do something new. A last bit of this season is trying to hold on, not quite ready to surrender to the life ahead. The pear trees are beginning to blossom now, but winter is still in my heart. I want to let go and prepare for better times. But it's cold outside. How can I warm myself on the inside while I wait? Spring will come. I know it will. It always does. But for now, I will rest in simple comforts. I will read my Word and call a friend for a visit to warm my heart.

Practical Matters

It has been a long journey. We sometimes feel as if we have been snowed in for a long winter. So much healing has taken place, though. And new life is beginning to sprout fresh green shoots through the hard, cold ground. Here it comes—what you have waited for. Many transitions between seasons will happen on this journey. What you do in the transition determines how well you move through the next season. Try not to run ahead before it is time. Go back to what comforts and strengthens you, simple things like reading your Word daily and enjoying small pleasures. As your energy returns, let yourself think about the next season. God's plans for your future are at work in your imagination. Dream a little ….

Word Strength

"For I know the plans I have for you," says the Lord. "They are plans for good and not for disaster, to give you a future and a hope" (Jeremiah 29:11 NLT).

Prayer

It has been a long cold winter, my Shepherd. I feel a change inside, along with signs of spring outside my window. Oh, I'm so ready! Stir new life within me, Jesus. Renew my hope for the season ahead. Let the wonderful plans you have for me lead me into your dreams for my life. I want to clean out the clutter of the dead winter and experience the colorful warm breezes of new life. Amen.

Come to the Table

Journal Entry

I saw my table today. I have focused lately on fighting enemies of fear and anxiety. Then I read the words in the Psalm, saying the Lord prepares a table before me in the presence of my enemies. I thought about such a table. If it were my unique place with my favorite things, what would it look like? I like rustic mixed with lace. So I imagine my table would be a heavy, chunky round surface spread with a simple European-lace runner. It would be set with earth-toned pottery, complete with wooden-handled utensils and a teapot and mugs. A fresh bouquet of fragrant mountain flowers would adorn the center. Now for the food. I think the Shepherd would know all my favorites: chocolate mousse—he would let me eat dessert first!—mashed potatoes, green beans, and Texas chicken-fried steak with gravy. Yum! I like my table.

Practical Matters

What does your table look like? I believe it is a specific place, unique to what the Shepherd knows about you, your likes, and dislikes. I imagine the food is heavenly in taste and nutrition. And of course, you never gain a pound! Take a break from the worries of your day and use your imagination to journal about your table. Let the Shepherd feed your soul with his goodness. He cares about what brings you joyful refreshment.

Word Strength

"You prepare a table before me in the presence of my enemies;
You anoint my head with oil;
My cup runs over" (Psalm 23:5).

Prayer

Jesus, I want to take a break with you. Would you show me what my table looks like? It amazes me that right here, in the middle of my battles, you prepare a table for me. I want to sit with you for a while and just enjoy knowing how much you care for me. As I close my eyes, I picture your provisions in my life. I receive a fresh anointing as you pour oil on my head. My cup runs over with the blessings of your love for me.

Loneliness

Journal Entry

I am trying to put on a brave and confident face to the world, but the truth is, I am *so* lonely. People are all around: friends, family, church family. But I feel lonely in each crowd and when I am by myself. It never seems to end. I miss having someone to talk to at the end of the day. I miss having someone to hold my hand or steady my racing thoughts. I miss the sound of his voice, his warm embrace. It is a hollow place that no one can fill. I am tempted to reach out for a companion. Someone actually asked me on a date, and I cringed. No, that's not what I want either. Not yet. So today I asked the Shepherd what to do. I said, "I know you are with me all the time, but I need someone with skin on. Can you help, Jesus? I don't want to settle for less just because I don't want to be alone. I lean into your companionship during this isolated season. Please be more real than you've ever been and hold me steady."

Practical Matters

Loneliness is treacherous but offers a great opportunity for love. Many people in the valley have never really been alone before, especially if they have lost a spouse. This can be a dangerous place because it is new and intense. Every moment spent alone can press on your heart with the reality that your loved one is actually gone. You might be tempted to avoid that feeling. But you need to embrace it. Yes, embrace it. You can gain the wonderful blessing and amazing experience of knowing *yourself* as you battle through loneliness.

Learn to become comfortable with yourself. When you are forced to surrender, you will find a greater acceptance of who God created you to be. You are *not* alone. Allow the Shepherd to draw close and show you the reality of his companionship. His presence is healing. Press into it. He will show up and not disappoint you. You will love getting to know him in this place. I promise, you do not want to miss it. In the process, he will reveal the loving wonders of who you are. And who knows? This experience might be the very thing that makes you ready for another companion in the days ahead. I always say that if you are good alone, you can be good together because you know and love yourself very well.

Word Strength

"Where can I go from Your Spirit?
Or where can I flee from Your presence?
If I ascend into heaven, You are there;
If I make my bed in hell, behold, You are there.
If I take the wings of the morning,
And dwell in the uttermost parts of the sea,
Even there Your hand shall lead me,
And Your right hand shall hold me.
If I say, "Surely the darkness shall fall on me,"
Even the night shall be light about me;
Indeed, the darkness shall not hide from You,
But the night shines as the day;
The darkness and the light are both alike to You" (Psalm 139:7–12).

"I will praise You, for I am fearfully and wonderfully made;
Marvelous are Your works,
And that my soul knows very well.
My frame was not hidden from You,
When I was made in secret,
And skillfully wrought in the lowest parts of the earth.

Your eyes saw my substance, being yet unformed.

And in Your book they all were written,

The days fashioned for me,

When as yet there were none of them.

How precious also are Your thoughts to me, O God!

How great is the sum of them!

If I should count them, they would be more in number than the sand;

When I awake, I am still with You" (Psalm 139:14–18).

Prayer

My Shepherd, I feel lonely today. I'm not sure what to do about it. But your Word says that I can't escape from your presence. So would you come near and help me recognize your companionship as you soothe the ache in my soul? I need you now! I lean into your love. Teach me how to be alone with you. I'm yours. Amen.

Resurrection Power

Journal Entry

Something is a little different today. I am looking for some light in the darkness. My heart feels a strange combination of dull tiredness and emerging hope, like little flickers of light in the distance ahead of me. I have a sense of compassionate power surging around and within me. Oh, my goodness! I just realized that today is Easter Sunday. I understand now. I feel the Shepherd's strength. Thank you, Lord, for understanding this journey so personally. I can feel your compassion for me as you identify with my suffering. I also feel your resurrection power, more real to me than ever before. I have always loved Easter. But here in this valley, it is everything I hope for. Easter is real. And I am feeling this reality today. I am so thankful, Lord, for your death-conquering love.

Practical Matters

The darkness of the tomb might be all you see for a time and feels like nothing but pain, despair, and loss. Jesus experienced this himself after the crucifixion. He knew how the tomb felt: the loss, the devastation, the end of all things. We might think that he knew what was coming in the resurrection, so he didn't experience death like we do. But he did. He felt all the deep realities of his own death, knowing that one day, he would walk you through the valley.

How much power do you think it will take to get you through this? Sometimes it's hard to imagine that kind of power exists. But the same Spirit that raised Christ from the dead lives inside you. This incredible power is at work in you right now to bring life out of death. Let the wonder of the Holy Spirit within begin to stir in you now. Be aware of his presence and surrender to his loving work as he leads you step-by-step out of the darkness of the tomb and into resurrection light.

Word Strength

"But if the same Spirit of Him who raised Jesus from the dead dwells in you, He who raised Christ from the dead will also give life to your mortal bodies through His Spirit who dwells in you" (Romans 8:11).

Prayer

Lord Jesus, thank you for the experience of your compassionate power. It means so much to me to know that you understand how I feel. But you do not just understand; you did something about it. You conquered death once and for all so that even in this place of goodbye, I can stand in the light of your victory. Holy Spirit, come, live in me and stir new life and vitality in my spirit, soul, and body.

Be Very Strong and Courageous

Journal Entry

Today in my quiet time, the Shepherd led me to Joshua 1:9. Moses had just died, and Joshua was being prepared by God to lead the people across the Jordan River into the promised land. He said to him, "Have I not commanded you? Be strong and of good courage; Do not be afraid, nor be dismayed for the Lord your God is with you wherever you go." Joshua was grieving the loss of his spiritual father, Moses, and confronted with the task of leading the people on a seemingly impossible journey to a new land. Today I feel the same way. I feel the loss of my husband and best friend so deeply. I look at our future with trembling uncertainty. I feel as if I am preparing to lead my family across a treacherous river into a new land. So today I make a decision. Although I feel weak, wounded, and overwhelmed, I will turn that verse into a grateful declaration. Lord, I thank you that I am strong. I thank you that I am courageous. I do not have to be afraid; I do not have to be afraid. Thank you that you have promised to be with me wherever I go. I am not alone. I will be very strong and courageous.

Practical Matters

Very strong and courageous? Now? The way I feel today? Yes, now. Today, in the middle of your trembling uncertainty. Hear the Lord saying to you, "Do not be afraid, nor dismayed for the Lord your God is with you wherever you go." A new level of strength and courage is deep down inside you that you might not have tapped into before. But it is there. Use your own mouth to speak to your heart and watch it rise up within you.

Word Strength

"Have I not commanded you? Be strong and of good courage; do not be afraid, nor be dismayed, for the Lord your God is with you wherever you go" (Joshua 1:9).

Prayer

Lord, I thank you that I am strong. I thank you that I am courageous. I do not have to be afraid; I do not have to be afraid. Thank you that you have promised to be with me wherever I go. I am not alone. I will be very strong and courageous.

Beauty for Ashes

Journal Entry

The last few months have been all about exchanges. I have identified some hard personal traits on my way: my own self-centeredness, stubborn will, tendencies toward isolation, and orphan heartedness. I can see how easy it is for me to go about my life, wearing either the ashes of grief or religious superiority. Both are a cover up of the true me. I feel a readiness to let go of my pride and bow low before my Maker so that he can take from me the old ways of doing life in exchange for the wholeness he purchased for me on the cross.

Practical Matters

What about you? Look back at the list of blessings and dangers in the valley. Is there anything you feel ready to exchange: love for fear, compassionate truth for self-pity, life for death? The work of Christ in us is always about exchanging the little we have for the great gifts he secured for us in his death and resurrection. He conquered death so that you could recover from your loss and receive the many blessings of your salvation: health, loving relationships, provision, protection, peace, and renewed joy. Listen again to a portion of his mission statement and let your heart respond as he nudges you.

Word Strength

"The Spirit of the Lord God is upon Me,
Because the Lord has anointed Me …
To comfort all who mourn,
To console those who mourn in Zion,
To give them beauty for ashes,

The oil of joy for mourning,

The garment of praise for the spirit of heaviness;

That they may be called trees of righteousness,

The planting of the Lord, that He may be glorified"(Isaiah 61:1–3).

Prayer

Lord, thank you for all the blessings of life you purchased for me on the cross. Today I exchange (fill in the blank with what you want to release) for (fill in the blank with what you want to receive). I give you my ashes and receive beauty. I release to you a little more of my mourning journey and receive an anointing of joy. I take off heaviness as you place around me a garment of praise. Let my roots go deep in your love so that this life brings you glory. Amen.

My Cup Overflows

You anoint my head with oil;
My cup overflows (Psalm 23:5 ESV).

The River

Journal Entry

Today I went for a walk and talked to the river. It has been such a long time.

My dear old friend, what times we have had. I have seen you in times of fullness when the rains swelled you beyond your capacity. I rested my feet in the cool refreshing of your flow on a hot day. We even shared days of dryness when we were both parched and crying out for the rains to come. And when they came, we danced together, splashing in happy delight. We share the babbling sounds of praise—my favorite!—that rise as together, we enjoy the presence of our Creator.

Oh, my friend, I am so happy to see you. The last time I saw you, you were broken, filled with silt and debris from the raging forest flames. You now know all too well the realities of death and life. Ah, but you are restored. Look at you. The landscape around you is quite changed. You move on with fresh energy, creating new life wherever you go. Your banks are green and lush. The birds sing in the thickets, and the deer rest on the cool banks. Now you are clean. Your resources rush forth from the depths of the Creator's love. Life goes on. You are beautifully revived.

Oh! I am so happy to see you!

Practical Matters

Restoration is so beautiful. New growth is beginning to bud on the banks of your life. Only you and the Shepherd know the devastation that preceded this new landscape and how great a miracle it is that you are here now, fully alive. Take time to explore this new place. Walk with him along the banks and look closely at the new growth. Become acquainted with how life looks and feels here in this place. Remember, this river flows from the very sanctuary of heaven. The heart of God is here, moving you into his loving plans. He has supplied all that you need for the new season. Take your nourishment from the tree of life. Its healing leaves are all around you.

Word Strength

"Fruit trees of all kinds will grow along both sides of the river. The leaves of these trees will never turn brown and fall, and there will always be fruit on their branches. There will be a new crop every month, for they are watered by the river flowing from the Temple. The fruit will be for food and the leaves for healing" (Ezekiel 47:12 NLT).

Prayer

Precious Shepherd, here we are, standing by this beautiful river. I see life all around me now, and I am so grateful. Thank you for new growth that is real and freshly full of potential. It emerges within my own heart. Help me be aware of it more and more every day. I will choose to observe your loving work in my life and receive refreshment from the riverbank often. Amen.

Awakenings

Journal Entry

Time to wake up again. My daddy used to say, "Wake up! Wake up, baby girl. It's a new day." For so long, I struggled to wake up in the mornings. They were a sober reckoning with another day on the journey of mourning. But now, when I see the morning sun peek through the window, I feel happier than I have in a long time. A sense of anticipation, a bright light, is growing in my heart. I see beyond my grief into the present and ongoing events of this one day. The sun has come up over the hill of my pain, and I am grateful for a new day. I know that my loved ones are standing in the brightness of the Son of God. They are rejoicing today in the full knowledge of his goodness and love ... and so can I.

Practical Matters

Take time to notice how you are feeling. Are you experiencing some better days and moods? Write about this. Put words to your emotions. Share them with the Shepherd in gratitude and continued surrender. The new places can be very much like waking up in a new land. And you are. You are making it through the valley to the other side. Enjoy the moments when your heart beats in a comfortable rhythm again. Wake up to new life discoveries and enjoy the moments of happiness. Suffering always brings glory. So let the glory of the Lord rise in your heart. Others will see it as well and celebrate your awakening journey.

Word Strength

"Arise, shine;
For your light has come!
And the glory of the Lord is risen upon you.

For behold, the darkness shall cover the earth,

And deep darkness the people;

But the Lord will arise over you,

And His glory will be seen upon you" (Isaiah 60:1–2).

Prayer

Lord, I hear you calling me to "arise and shine, for your light has come." I say yes, Lord, to your call. Let your light come. Let your glory rise in my life. Thank you for this new place, for the ability to feel new life and light in my heart. I will never forget how far we've come on this trek through the valley, and neither will you. We are forever bound together by the cords of shared suffering. But that is not all that binds us. The shared joyful awakenings are greater than I could have ever dreamed possible. I respond to your call, rising up in the light, putting names to these feelings, and moving into the next steps of this light-filled life.

Old Clothes

Journal Entry

A fresh new dress makes you feel pretty. I've worn all kinds of clothes on this journey. Some were drab and sad while others were an awkward attempt to feel okay. Sometimes I felt very out of place in my own clothes, like nothing really fit right anymore. I try to be me, but even that is changing. I want to be pretty, but who am I being pretty for now that my husband isn't here to see me? I think it's time to clean out my closet again, to let some clothes go. Mourning garments can't be given to the second-hand store for someone else to wear. That just feels wrong. They should be put in the sea of forgetfulness and released, replaced with vibrant, living fibers for a new day. I think I'll get dressed again and go shopping.

Practical Matters

Some days, you will probably feel you are ready for something new. I am not talking about shopping for comfort and impulsively spending money. I am talking about a time to refresh yourself in a practical way. Enjoy the moment. Do something simple or even big. Buy a new outfit or new shoes or get a haircut. It is a sign that you are moving forward in your new life. Enjoy!

Word Strength

"You have turned for me my mourning into dancing;

You have put off my sackcloth and clothed me with gladness,

To the end that my glory may sing praise to You and not be silent.

O Lord my God, I will give thanks to You forever" (Psalm 30:11–12).

Prayer

Beautiful Shepherd, it feels strange to feel better again, but I know it is so healthy. I am ready to put away some of my grieving garments and let you clothe me in new joy and gladness. Show me what I need to let go of in my closet and heart. Guide my steps as I walk toward new places of life. Help me to take joy in simple things, always with my eyes on you, my decisions firmly rooted in your leadership. And at the end of this day, may my praise rise to you in joyful expectation.

Tears in a Bottle

Journal Entry

Lord, I've cried and cried! I've cried so much that I feel exhausted and dehydrated. Just when I think the streams might slow a bit, another wave comes, and the floods begin again. How many tears must I cry? How many is enough? Where do they all go anyway? Your Word says that you keep my tears in a bottle. (See Psalm 56:8.) Why would you save them all? Oh, I'm tired of crying! Shepherd, what do you do with all my tears? "I gather them in my heart and yours, turning them into living water. When the time is right, you and I will pour them out for others who need them."

Practical Matters

Your tears, my friend, are more precious than you know. They are salt water from your weary eyes. But they are so much more. Each one is a supernatural seed you are sowing in the Shepherd's heart. You are healing, and the seeds are growing into a stream of living water. No, you will not cry forever. You will feel better than this. When you feel weepy, take a little extra time to rest. Let the tears fall for a bit, and then wash your face, drink a glass of water, and shift your focus. Simply change rooms, or go outside for a bit. A change of scenery and a little movement will help your energy return.

Word Strength

"You keep track of all my sorrows.
You have collected all my tears in your bottle.
You have recorded each one in your book" (Psalm 56:8 NLT).

Prayer

Jesus, I thank you for caring so deeply about my pain. You know every sad beat of my heart, so I lean into your comforting love today. All I have to give you are my tears. But your Word says you know and have recorded each one. That is more than I can understand. I trust that you know what to do with them and that you will turn them into living water in the days ahead.

Milestones

Journal Entry

Yesterday was Father's Day. It seems like every time I turn around, another anniversary or holiday reminds me of my loss. Birthdays and watermarks of our life together keep washing over me like unwelcome swells of harsh sea water. This first year was really rough. I'm not sure how we endured these days. Sometimes we went into hiding and pretended they were not happening, just waiting for them to pass. Attempts to celebrate in special ways seem valuable but always bittersweet, leaving me with an achy dullness. I so wish I could do something magical for my family to ease the pain. The dreadful anticipation of each anniversary or holiday can be agonizing. I think about it way ahead of a time, imagining many scenarios. The sorrowful butterflies multiply in my stomach as each day moves us closer. When the dreaded day finally arrives, we move on. The anticipation of it seems to be the worst part, like squeezing through a narrow passage I barely fit through.

Practical Matters

The narrow trails leading into special days are challenging but very important steps to healing. Every time you squeeze through the tight and tender passage of time, you move through a corridor of restoration. Do what you can. If you are able to do something special to remember your loved one, do it. Tell funny stories, go to their favorite restaurant for dinner, create art that honors what you enjoyed about them. Talk to the Shepherd about it too. He understands and will give you creative steps forward. Hold tight to him. He knows how to position you just right to fit successfully through each gate. As you go through each one, look back and remember how far you have come on your journey, and deliberately celebrate God's faithfulness in your shaky steps.

Word Strength

"When I remember You on my bed,
I meditate on You in the night watches.
Because You have been my help,
Therefore in the shadow of Your wings I will rejoice.
My soul follows close behind You;
Your right hand upholds me" (Psalm 63:6–8).

Prayer

Another special day is approaching, Lord. They seem to come way too often. What can I do to celebrate well without causing unnecessary pain? Would you lead me through this passage? You are still here with me, and I am still here with you. I am trusting in you once again. Thank you, God, for showing me the way as I follow close behind you. Amen.

Joy Splash

Journal Entry

Shepherd, you are so precious to me, so glorious, so beautiful. I trust you more than ever. Today I am eager for new beginnings responding to the energies of transformation. I feel special, not special because I'm sad, but special because I have come to know the love of Jesus intimately in the valley. I am walking in the stream of your strength. The water level is rising. I find a deep river inside me. Trying to capture it is like scooping out the water with a thimble. The current is strong, and the banks are beginning to overflow. It's a joy splash with swirls of magnificent living color, clothing me in grace and new dignity. My confidence rises as I stand surrounded by your glory. I'm not afraid. I'm diving in.

Practical Matters

New life is flowing deep inside you. Even when you are overwhelmed, you have no reason for apprehension. This new flow of life is the result of your journey to believe in the goodness of the Shepherd's heart. Talk with him about what's happening. He will teach you how to walk in the new places of his Spirit life through his Word. Most of all, enjoy the river. Take off your shoes and wade into the living water. Dance, swirl, enjoy the joy splash in your heart.

Word Strength

"He who believes in Me, as the Scripture has said, out of his heart will flow rivers of living water" (John 7:38).

Prayer

Thank you, beautiful God, for this river flowing inside me. I believe in your goodness, Shepherd. Thank you for the work of your Holy Spirit within me. I ask you to teach me how to walk and swim here in your glory. I will joyfully trust your leadership in days ahead. Let the river flow. Amen.

Goodness and Mercy

Surely goodness and mercy will follow me
All the days of my life;
And I will dwell in the house of the Lord
Forever (Psalm 23:6).

Divine Kisses

Journal Entry

Everything seems to be coming together. It has been a rocky path through this valley. Most of the time, I couldn't see how the tapestry of my life was weaving together. Honestly, it took great faith to keep believing in what I could not see. But now that my heart feels better, I have a broader view of it all. I can take a step back from my own self-focus and see the divine convergence of blessings that have found their way to meet right in the center of my heart. Love, goodness, mercy, truth, righteousness, peace, and wisdom are colliding as new life emerges from me. How amazing!

Practical Matters

The gift of perspective will return if you look for it. Actively take a step back on occasion. Try to see your story from an outsider's point of view. You might try writing a letter to yourself in third person as a friend writing to another friend. Point out what you observed in the journey. Be specific. Speak words of encouragement and hope for the future. Talk about where you have seen the Shepherd bring circumstances together. Celebrate your accomplishments in recovery. Then read the letter aloud. You might be amazed at what comes into view.

Word Strength

"Mercy and truth have met together;
Righteousness and peace have kissed" (Psalm 85:10).

Prayer

Wonderful God, you are bringing powerful aspects of your character together in my life. I pray for great awareness of these divine kisses in the center of my heart. Shift my focus where I need new perspective. Thank you for your kind leadership in my life. Amen.

Travel Light

Journal Entry

Today I pack my bags for Africa. I can't believe I get to go. This whole journey has been a big adventure. Sometimes I felt as if I were on safari surrounded by lions. I can't wait to see the African sunrise and meet new people. But I have to travel light. I know from experience, I don't want to carry any more weight than necessary. Hopping on and off trains, planes, and automobiles can be exhilarating unless you carry too much stuff. If you do, it's a burden. I want to stay in the moment, focused on one leg of the trip at a time. Oh, I am so ready for a new adventure. God is so much fun. I take with me only what I need, a determination to live in the moment and deep trust in my Shepherd who created every landscape of my life.

Practical Matters

It is time to clean out your bags. Get rid of all the smelly, wrinkled clothes; trash; and old mindsets. You have gained lots of new supplies for life to sustain you as you move on from the valley. Keep only what adds to your life: a closer relationship with the Shepherd, new understanding of yourself, reordered priorities, compassion, and deep joy. Ask the Shepherd to show you anything you need to unpack. He will help you. Now that you know how precious time is, prepare to stay current, living in the fullness of each day. Travel light. New adventures await, and God has surprises planned for you. You are going to love it.

Word Strength

"Come to Me, all you who labor and are heavy laden, and I will give you rest. Take My yoke upon you and learn from Me, for I am gentle and lowly in heart, and you will find rest for your souls. For My yoke is easy and My burden is light" (Matthew 11:28–30).

Prayer

Lord, it feels good to unpack my bags after this long journey. I am not sure what I need for the next part, but I know I want to lighten the load and put away old things. I ask you to show me what to keep and what to let go of. I will take the best memories of my loved one and everything you taught me through the valley. I give you every burden and come up under your yoke. It is light, and your strength supports me. I will travel light and live life in your rest. Amen.

Taste and See

Journal Entry

My senses are coming back. You learn to appreciate the small changes on this journey. I am more keenly aware of so many things. It seems as if everything was dull for so long. Nothing tasted good, smelled right, or sounded clear. But now the dullness has lifted from my physical and spiritual senses. They have grown sharper on this road. I am beginning to enjoy my surroundings again. Like a toddler exploring her new world, I want to see and hear and feel and taste everything.

Practical Matters

Are your senses coming back to life? Give yourself permission to be aware of it. It is a great sign that you are healing. Enjoy the new sensations. Just take it one step at a time as the Shepherd leads you. Share your life with your community. Renew friendships. And let the Lord show you all the tastes, sights, and sounds he has for you now. You have a new capacity to choose and delight in wonderful things. Nothing can compare to the sweetness of his loving plans for you. So enjoy this part of the journey, trusting his guidance in new places.

Word Strength

I will bless the Lord at all times;
His praise shall continually be in my mouth.
My soul shall make its boast in the Lord;
The humble shall hear of it and be glad.
Oh, magnify the Lord with me,
And let us exalt His name together.
I sought the Lord, and He heard me,

And delivered me from all my fears.
They looked to Him and were radiant,
And their faces were not ashamed.
This poor man cried out, and the Lord heard him,
And saved him out of all his troubles.
The angel of the Lord encamps all around those who fear Him,
And delivers them.
Oh, taste and see that the Lord is good;
Blessed is the man who trusts in Him! (Psalm 34:1–8).

Prayer

Oh, Lord, my heart is full of praise and wonder. I have tasted your goodness over and over again. That is more than I could have ever asked for. Now my senses are coming back, and I taste and see so many things. I want to experience life again. I will stay close by your side. Hold my hand, Shepherd. Keep me steady. Open the eyes of my heart. I am ready to see all you have for me in the seasons ahead. Amen.

A New Thing

Journal Entry

I love the places in my Bible where God promises to make things new. They feel very real to me now, like a steady current, carrying me forward in time. As I ride along on their momentum, my faith is strengthened, and I hope for promises fulfilled and for new things still developing. The creation of new pathways and rivers takes time. It is an ongoing flow of my life in the hands of the Master Craftsman.

Practical Matters

The Lord is doing new things for you. Do you see it? Actually, he was working all along the way, carving new rivers and roads in your heart. They are beautiful new features you have never seen before. Take time to look closely at these new things. You might need to stop looking back at the old people, places, and things of the past season. That is how you move into the new. Everything that has happened to you in your life is shaping who you are now. Trust the Shepherd to blend it all together. Only he knows how the pieces fit. Surrender to the new. You will be glad you did.

Word Strength

"For I am about to do something new.
See, I have already begun! Do you not see it?
I will make a pathway through the wilderness.
I will create rivers in the dry wasteland" (Isaiah 43:19 NLT).

Prayer

Master Creator, I want to perceive what you are doing as you create new things in my life. Thank you for every promise made to me, for every pathway, and every river flowing. Help me to see what you are doing. I want to join you in your work. Something in me loves making things new. I must be a little like my Shepherd.

My Soul's Celebration

Today I remember all the benefits of my relationship with the Shepherd. His goodness has overwhelmed me. I always loved the words of Psalm 103. Now as I finish writing this book for you, my fellow traveler, I share from *The Passion Translation*. These words describe my response to the valley journey better than I ever could. I applaud your journey, dear friend. Thank you for allowing me to travel along with you for a while. Let's lift this prayer together in celebration of God's faithfulness on our healing road.

> With my whole heart, with my whole life,
> and with my innermost being,
> I bow in wonder and love before you, the holy God!
> Yahweh, you are my soul's celebration.
> How could I ever forget the miracles of kindness
> you've done for me?
> You kissed my heart with forgiveness, in spite of all I've done.
> You've healed me inside and out from every disease.
> You've rescued me from hell and saved my life.
> You've crowned me with love and mercy.
> You satisfy my every desire with good things.
> You've supercharged my life so that I soar again
> like a flying eagle in the sky!
> You're a God who makes things right,
> giving justice to the defenseless.
> You unveiled to Moses your plans
> and showed Israel's sons what you could do.
> Lord, you're so kind and tenderhearted
> to those who don't deserve it
> and so patient with people who fail you!
> Your love is like a flooding river

overflowing its banks with kindness.
You don't look at us only to find our faults,
just so that you can hold a grudge against us.
You may discipline us for our many sins,
but never as much as we really deserve.
Nor do you get even with us for what we've done.
Higher than the highest heavens—
that's how high your tender mercy extends!
Greater than the grandeur of heaven above
is the greatness of your loyal love, towering over all
who fear you and bow down before you!
Farther than from a sunrise to a sunset—
that's how far you've removed our guilt from us.
The same way a loving father feels toward his children—
that's but a sample of your tender feelings toward us,
your beloved children, who live in awe of you.
You know all about us, inside and out.
You are mindful that we're made from dust.
Our days are so few, and our momentary beauty
so swiftly fades away!
Then all of a sudden we're gone,
like grass clippings blown away in a gust of wind,
taken away to our appointment with death,
leaving nothing to show that we were here.
But Lord, your endless love stretches
from one eternity to the other,
unbroken and unrelenting toward those who fear you
and those who bow facedown in awe before you.
Your faithfulness to keep every gracious promise you've made
passes from parents, to children, to grandchildren, and beyond.
You are faithful to all those who follow your ways

and keep your word.
God's heavenly throne is eternal, secure, and strong,
and his sovereignty rules the entire universe.
So bless the Lord, all his messengers of power,
for you are his mighty heroes who listen intently
to the voice of his word to do it.
Bless and praise the Lord, you mighty warriors,
ministers who serve him well and fulfill his desires.
I will bless and praise the Lord with my whole heart!
Let all his works throughout the earth,
wherever his dominion stretches,
let everything bless the Lord! (Psalm 103 TPT).

ABOUT THE AUTHOR

Mary Kay McCauley Stone has a passion to see people discover their true destiny in Christ. She has more than thirty years of full-time ministry experience, including pastoral care and counseling, cross-cultural evangelism, teaching, and prayer leadership. She is a certified life coach and biblical Counselor. She is the founder and director of Quest Restoration Ministries, where she and her husband Doug serve as life coaches. She enjoys spending time with her three grown sons and their families, including seven grandchildren.